OECD e-Governmen

The e-Government Imperative

OECD

ORGANISATION FOR ECONOMIC CO-OPERATION AND DEVELOPMENT

ORGANISATION FOR ECONOMIC CO-OPERATION AND DEVELOPMENT

Pursuant to Article 1 of the Convention signed in Paris on 14th December 1960, and which came into force on 30th September 1961, the Organisation for Economic Co-operation and Development (OECD) shall promote policies designed:

- to achieve the highest sustainable economic growth and employment and a rising standard of living in member countries, while maintaining financial stability, and thus to contribute to the development of the world economy;
- to contribute to sound economic expansion in member as well as non-member countries in the process of economic development; and
- to contribute to the expansion of world trade on a multilateral, non-discriminatory basis in accordance with international obligations.

The original member countries of the OECD are Austria, Belgium, Canada, Denmark, France, Germany, Greece, Iceland, Ireland, Italy, Luxembourg, the Netherlands, Norway, Portugal, Spain, Sweden, Switzerland, Turkey, the United Kingdom and the United States. The following countries became members subsequently through accession at the dates indicated hereafter: Japan (28th April 1964), Finland (28th January 1969), Australia (7th June 1971), New Zealand (29th May 1973), Mexico (18th May 1994), the Czech Republic (21st December 1995), Hungary (7th May 1996), Poland (22nd November 1996), Korea (12th December 1996) and the Slovak Republic (14th December 2000). The Commission of the European Communities takes part in the work of the OECD (Article 13 of the OECD Convention).

Publié en français sous le titre :
L'administration électronique : un impératif

Foreword

While most studies of e-government focus on the provision of online services, OECD countries have emphasised that reforming the back office is just as fundamental to achieving effective government as updating front office service delivery channels. By focussing on the challenges and obstacles that must be overcome for successful e-government, and on the importance of co-ordination and collaboration between agencies for seamless service delivery, "The E-Government Imperative" provides a unique perspective on the problems facing governments today when implementing e-government. The report is intended as a practical tool for decision makers.

Ministers from OECD countries recognised the importance of e-government at their annual meeting in June 2001 as a major enabler of good governance practices. This report, based on the work of the OECD E-Government Working Group, identifies how governments can embed good governance principles into solutions that exploit 21st century information and communications technologies (ICTs) to achieve public policy goals within a context of changing social, economic and political circumstances.

The report was written by Tim Field, Elizabeth Muller and Edwin Lau of the OECD E-Government Task Force of the Public Governance and Territorial Development Directorate. Hélène Gadriot-Renard and Christian Vergez are the co-ordinators of the Project. The report was prepared under the direction of the E-Government Working Group and the OECD Public Management Committee, and is published on the responsibility of the Secretary-General of the OECD.

Acknowledgements

The Secretariat would like to thank all countries that provided information and/or participated in the OECD E-Government Seminars, 2002. In particular we would like to thank the members of the OECD E-Government Working Group (Australia, Canada, Denmark, Finland, France, Germany, Italy, Japan, Korea, Mexico, Netherlands, United States) for their input and constant support of this project.

Thanks are also due to Joanne Caddy, Marco Daglio, Christina Lagdameo and Maria Tapia, who helped draft sections of the report, and Liz Dacier who helped with the collection of the country examples. Finally, a special mention to Marie Murphy, Elaine Newton and many others, without whose support this report would never have been published.

Table of Contents

List of Boxes

List of Figures

THE E-GOVERNMENT IMPERATIVE – ISBN 92-64-10117-9 – © OECD 2003

Executive Summary

Introduction

E-government is more about government than about "e"

The rise of the information society has led to major changes in citizen expectations and organisational structures, cultures and working processes. Governments will have to follow suite and adopt information society tools and working practices if they are to remain responsive to citizen needs. The OECD defines "e-government" as "the use of information and communication technologies, and particularly the Internet, as a tool to achieve better government". The impact of e-government at the broadest level is simply **better government** by enabling better policy outcomes, higher quality services, greater engagement with citizens and by improving other key outputs identified. Governments and public administrations will, and should, continue to be judged against these established criteria for success.

E-government initiatives refocus attention on a number of issues: how to collaborate more effectively across agencies to address complex, shared problems; how to enhance customer focus; and how to build relationships with private sector partners. Public administrations must address these issues if they are to remain responsive.

The case for E-government

E-government improves efficiency

ICTs enable **efficiency improvements** in mass processing tasks and public administration operations. Internet-based applications can generate savings on data collection and transmission, provision of information and communication with customers. Significant future efficiencies are likely through greater sharing of data within and between governments.

E-government improves services

Adopting a customer focus is a core element of member countries' reform agendas. Successful services (both online and off line) are built on an understanding of user requirements. A customer focus means implies that a user should not have to understand complex government structures and relationships in order to interact with government. The Internet can help achieve this goal, by enabling governments to appear as a unified organisation and provide **seamless online service**. As with all services, e-government services must be developed in light of demand and user value, as part of an overall service channel strategy.

E-government helps achieve specific policy outcomes...

The Internet can help stakeholders share information and ideas and thus contribute to specific **policy outcomes.** For example, online information can boost use of an educational or training programme; sharing of information in the health sector can improve resource use and patient care; and sharing of information between central and sub-national governments can facilitate environmental policies. The sharing of information on individuals, however, will raise privacy protection issues, and the potential trade-offs need to be carefully assessed. Timeframes for initiatives need to be realistic, as there can be considerable lags before benefits accrue.

... and can contribute to economic policy objectives

E-government's facilitation of reduced corruption, greater openness and trust in government contributes to **economic policy objectives**. Specific impacts include the reduced government call on funds through more effective programmes, and efficiencies and improvements in business productivity (through ICT enabled administrative simplification and enhanced government information). Given the reach and influence of government, e-government initiatives act to promote Information Society and e-commerce objectives. Government consumption of ICT products and services can also support local ICT industries. However, impacts in these areas are difficult to quantify.

E-government can be a major contributor to reform

All OECD governments are facing the issue of public management modernisation and reform. Developments – globalisation, new fiscal demands, changing societies and increasing customer expectations – mean that the **reform process must be continuous.** ICTs have underpinned reforms in many areas, for example by improving transparency, facilitating information sharing and highlighting internal inconsistencies.

E-government can help build trust between governments and citizens

Building trust between governments and citizens is fundamental to good governance. **ICT can help build trust** by enabling citizen engagement in the policy process, promoting open and accountable government and helping to prevent corruption. Furthermore, if limits and challenges are properly overcome, e-government can help an individual's voice to be heard in the mass debate. This can be done by harnessing ICT to encourage citizens to think constructively about public issues, applying technology to open up the policy process and adopting policies on information quality and accountability. Integration with offline tools is required, and few expect e-government arrangements to completely replace traditional methods of information provision, consultation and public participation in the foreseeable future.

External barriers to e-government

Legislative and regulatory barriers, financial barriers, technological barriers and the digital divide, among others, can impede the uptake of e-government. While internal obstacles (such as collaboration for seamless services) are important, external barriers need to be addressed on a whole of government basis in order to be overcome.

Legislative and regulatory barriers can impede the uptake of e-government

In order for e-government processes to be adopted, they must have the same standing as the equivalent paper processes. Additionally, current frameworks based on the assumption that agencies work alone (*e.g.* performance management, accountability frameworks and an interdiction of data sharing) inhibit collaboration. Privacy and security also need to be ensured before online services can advance. Complexity of requirements is another problem. Agencies may need clarification on what they can and cannot do, particularly in the areas of data security and technical standards. This clarification is particularly important in the case of small agencies.

Budgetary frameworks can restrict e-government initiatives

To finance seamless government services and shared infrastructure, budgetary regulations should **facilitate co-operative funding mechanisms** such as co-ordinated bids for new funds and the pooling of funds. Additionally, appropriate ICT expenditure should be treated as an investment, recognising future benefits and providing a degree of certainty for future funding. This would focus ICT spending on developing cost-effective solutions.

In many OECD countries, existing **budgetary arrangements act against** efficient e-government. Organisations need incentives for cross-organisational projects and tools for measuring returns on investment. This can be achieved through a government-wide approach to the assessment of e-government benefits and the sharing of savings.

Governments need to prepare for technological change

Sharing data across legacy systems, developing shared infrastructure and dealing with fast moving technological change can inhibit progress in putting e-government initiatives in place. These issues can also increase implementation and support costs and increase risk of failure. Such issues will not abate, but will continue to require attention as technologies change. E-government co-ordinators can facilitate agency efforts through the adoption of whole of government standards and software integration technologies and the development of shared middleware and other infrastructure. Broader approaches for adapting to emerging technologies include: technology neutral legislation and regulation; performance requirements rather than technical specifications when procuring new technologies; and increasingly looking to international co-operation to harmonise approaches.

The digital divide impedes the benefits of e-government

Online access has advantages that are impossible to replicate offline, such as the drawing together of information, independent search capacity and interactive policy consultation. However within OECD countries there are significant differences in access to ICTs and the Internet. Generally the most disadvantaged have the lowest levels of access, yet they also often have high levels of interaction with government (for example the unemployed). If these individuals cannot access e-government services, they will **miss out on many of its benefits.** Improved online access for the public at large will increase the pool of potential users of e-government services; in itself this justifies pursuing policies to reduce the digital divide.

Implementing e-government

E-government challenges existing ways of working

ICT needs to be incorporated into a package of modernisation, organisational change and related reforms (including greater teamwork, flexibility in working arrangements and remuneration and enhanced knowledge management practices) that challenge **public governance frameworks**. There will not be a single model of an e-government enabled organisation. E-government co-ordinators should use ICTs as a tool to facilitate change, and should not attempt to restructure public administrations around current technology.

E-government requires leadership

The leadership and enthusiasm of individuals and organisations has driven many e-government advances. Leadership requires consistent vision,

THE E-GOVERNMENT IMPERATIVE – ISBN 92-64-10117-9 – © OECD 2003

commitment and action. In the early stages of e-government, leadership is needed to gain acceptance of concepts, and to put implementation frameworks in place. At a more advanced stage, leadership is needed to manage change and sustain support for initiatives, especially as benefits may take time to emerge.

Indeed, leadership is necessary at all levels, from the political to the administrative. Political leadership makes e-government a priority and guides transformation by putting it in a broader context. Within administrations, leading implementers help translate political vision into an action plan.

Seamless government services will draw agencies closer together

Seamless government services require different agencies to work closely together. Their **collaboration** cannot be merely technical, but must involve a deeper engagement in terms of shared customers. As services become more complex (and expensive), collaboration will also be driven by the need for efficiency. E-government co-ordinators should facilitate planning for seamless services, fund catalyst projects, clarify data-sharing arrangements and address accountability issues. When current ways of working make it difficult for agencies to collaborate, barriers to co-operation need to be overcome.

Yet co-ordinators must resolve a central dilemma: how to capture the benefits of co-ordinated action and shared approaches while maintaining individual agency responsibility and accountability for operations and results. Approaches adopted include whole of government governance structures, interoperability standards, shared infrastructure and key pathfinder projects. Reviewing the requirements governing ICT use on a regular basis is required.

Managers need e-government skills

E-government increases the need for ICT-related skills in government. The skills required for e-government are **not simply technical**, as general managers also need broad skills to engage in the ICT decision-making process. Necessary skills include a basic technical understanding (IT literacy), but also an understanding of information management and the information society. Managers must be able to lead (and not be led by) the organisation's IT department and outside partners, and must be able to integrate the organisation's ICT strategy with its broader goals.

Furthermore, traditional management skills need to be updated and strengthened to deal with the impact of e-government. Additional competencies are needed in areas such as performance management, accountability frameworks, co-operation and collaboration across departments, and public-private partnerships. Governments should take steps to identify and ensure (through training or outsourcing) the skills needed for effective e-government.

E-government involves public-private partnerships

Working with the private sector is a feature of almost all e-government activity. Governments work with private partners to access skills and products, reduce risk, draw in private capital and integrate provision of government services with private-sector channels. More innovative arrangements, involving flexible, longer-term relationships with partners sharing risks and rewards, can help respond to changing technologies and opportunities. E-government co-ordinators, in collaboration with procurement authorities and key agencies, should develop an **e-government public-private partnership framework**. As part of this framework, an examination of audit and accountability arrangements covering ICT partnerships would be helpful.

Implementing e-government can be risky, expensive and difficult

Implementing e-government can be risky, expensive and difficult, and **requires change**. Organisations tend to resist pressures for change, leading to wasted opportunities and unnecessary expenditure. Development of e-government implementation is also hampered by ineffective project management, technology failures, problems of first mover disadvantage, funding discontinuities, and unrealistic political demands. When ICT projects go wrong, cost overruns and service delivery failures can be highly visible.

Monitoring and evaluation are essential to effective e-government

E-government implementers must **articulate the impacts and benefits** of initiatives in order to justify continued political and public support. Assessment should be realistic and within timeframes that are useful to decision-makers. Priority should be given to the assessment of demand, benefits and service quality. Assessing demand remains a major weakness in OECD countries' e-government programmes, and as services become more complex and expensive this issue will become increasingly important.

Conclusions and future challenges

Governments are under pressure...

Pressures will continue for governments to be responsive to social changes, find efficiencies and address concerns about security and privacy. Both citizens and businesses expect governments to adapt, and their expectations will grow as the information society becomes more widespread.

Governments must rise to the challenges of new technologies as these technologies continue to evolve. Decisions taken today will determine future capacity. The initial impressive visible results of e-government (government websites, a number of sophisticated transactional services, and the development of portals) contrast with the next stage of e-government, which requires the development of hidden infrastructure, connected back office arrangements, and more complex services. Greater collaboration across levels of government, higher funding levels and deeper organisational change will be needed. However, governments adapt slowly, and tend to treat the information revolution and e-government as only one among multiple challenges with which it is confronted.

... but must continue the e-government enabled reform process

The term "e-government", as used by the OECD E-Government Project, applies to the use of ICT as a tool *to achieve better government*. E-government is not about business as usual, but has a focus on using ICT to transform the structures, operations and, most importantly, the culture of government. Modernising government structures, governance frameworks and processes to meet the e-government imperative will have fundamental impacts on how services are delivered, how policies are developed and how public administrations operate. As the impact of e-government becomes more profound, governments will have to strike equilibrium between protecting citizens' rights and better meeting their needs with more efficient, integrated services and policy engagement processes. What starts as a technical exercise aimed at developing more responsive programs and services becomes an exercise in governance.

The Internet and related technologies have laid the groundwork for a richer sharing of information between government and citizens, and for the introduction of the much heralded "webbed" or non-hierarchical administration. While there is no single model of an e-government enabled organisation, and public administrations will continue to evolve as the use of ICTs deepen, e-government can create networks of information flow among the different parts of the administration, irrespective of legislative or administrative boundaries and/or hierarchies. In fact, one can question whether or not government agencies can maintain their current internal divisions and territories while trying to maintain a single, simple interface with the citizen through e-government. The need for collaboration also extends beyond central administrations to encompass local and regional levels of government. What may have commenced as a technical approach to enhanced services may result in seamless government, cutting across the boundaries that separate different structures and functions in the public administration, to provide a seamless interface to both users of services and to citizens.

Capturing the benefits of e-government will be difficult, and require coordinated action across the range of topics analysed in this report. The *Guiding Principles for E-government* below set out a framework for such future action.

THE E-GOVERNMENT IMPERATIVE – ISBN 92-64-10117-9 – © OECD 2003

GUIDING PRINCIPLES FOR SUCCESSFUL E-GOVERNMENT

Vision/political will

1. **Leadership and Commitment:** Leadership and commitment, at both political and administrative levels, are crucial to managing change. Committed leaders are required to deal with disruptive change, to persevere when benefits take time to emerge, to respond when things go wrong, and to establish visions and plans for the future.

2. **Integration:** E-government is an enabler, not an end in itself. It needs to be integrated into broader policy and service delivery goals, broader public management reform processes and broader information society activity.

Common frameworks/co-operation

3. **Inter-agency collaboration:** E-government is most effective when agencies work together in customer-focussed groupings of agencies. Agency managers need to be able to operate within common frameworks to ensure interoperability, maximise implementation efficiency and avoid duplication. Shared infrastructure needs to be developed to provide a framework for individual agency initiatives. Incentives can help encourage collaboration.

4. **Financing:** ICT spending, where appropriate, should be treated as an investment, with consideration of projected streams of returns. E-government requires a level of certainty of future funding to provide sustainability to projects, avoid wasting resources and gain maximum benefit from given funding levels. A central funding programme could help foster innovation and allow for key demonstration projects.

Customer focus

5. **Access:** Governments should pursue policies to improve access to online services. Many advantages of online government information and services are not replicable offline, so that those who lack access will be excluded unless action is taken.

6. **Choice:** Customers should have choice in the method of interacting with government, and the adoption of online services should not reduce choice. A principle of "no wrong door" to access the administration should be adopted. Services should be driven by an understanding of customer needs.

7. **Citizen engagement:** E-government information and services should be of high quality and engage citizens in the policy process. Information quality policies and feedback mechanisms will help maximise the usefulness of information provision and strengthen citizen participation.

8. **Privacy:** E-government should not be delivered at the expense of established expectations of privacy protection, and should be approached with the goal of protecting individual privacy.

Responsibility

9. **Accountability:** E-government can open up government and policy processes and enhance accountability. Accountability arrangements should ensure that it is clear who is responsible for shared projects and initiatives. Similarly, the use of private sector partnerships must not reduce accountability.

10. **Monitoring and evaluation:** Identifying the demand, costs, benefits and impacts of e-government is crucial if momentum is to be sustained. E-government implementers cannot expect support if they cannot articulate potential benefits.

ISBN 92-64-10117-9
The E-Government Imperative
© OECD 2003

Chapter 1

Objectives, Scope and Context

1.1. Introduction

This project takes as its basic premise that e-government provides the capacity to reform the way public administrations operate and can result in more customer-focused, responsive government. This requires overcoming major challenges. This publication examines the potential and impact of e-government and the changes required to maximise its benefits.

Governments are major users of information and communication technologies (ICTs). In OECD countries, government use of ICTs is now well established and an integral part of how governments do business. From an initial focus on mass processing tasks, using mainframe computers in areas such as collecting national statistics and processing taxation returns, government use of ICTs has widened to encompass a full range of technologies and applications. For almost a decade, governments have used Internet-based technologies, particularly the World Wide Web and e-mail. There is scarcely an aspect of government activity that does not involve the use of ICTs.

It would be surprising if this were not the case. ICTs have become a crucial element of national infrastructure, underpinning economic and social activity in all OECD countries. Given the scale of their activities and the diverse nature of their business across all forms of economic activity, governments have derived significant benefits from embracing ICTs. They have often been at the forefront in the adoption of specific applications and have used their scale and position in local markets to foster the development of ICT production industries.

Governments have embraced the Internet. The emergence of the Internet and parallel developments in processing capacity and data storage over the 1990s have significantly altered the environment for ICT use across society and in government. While the longer-term effects of this digital revolution are likely to be profound, these developments have already increased pressure on governments to perform and provided them the capacity to do so.

Governments were not immune to the attractions of what is now seen as the dot-com bubble. However, they now understand better that real value can be obtained through the use of ICT, but that the need for basic assessments of benefits and costs, risks and opportunities remains.

In response to these new capabilities, OECD governments have issued e-government strategies, set targets and established e-government co-ordination bodies. In a number of countries, e-government is the specific responsibility of a minister; in others, it is part of the information society or other ministerial responsibilities. These responses suggest that, primarily owing to the emergence of the Internet, there has been a qualitative shift in the role governments assign to ICTs. This parallels similar responses in the broader economy, where the Internet's potential had led to the information society and e-commerce policies, initiatives and co-ordinating structures.

1.2. Definitions

Defining e-government. There are many definitions of e-government, and the term itself is not universally used. The differences are not just semantic and may reflect priorities in government strategies. The definitions fall into three groups:

● E-government is defined as Internet (online) service delivery and other Internet-based activity such as e-consultation.

● E-government is equated to the use of ICTs in government. While the focus is generally on the delivery of services and processing, the broadest definition encompasses all aspects of government activity.

● E-government is defined as a capacity to transform public administration through the use of ICTs or indeed is used to describe a new form of government built around ICTs. This aspect is usually linked to Internet use.

Definitions and terms adopted by individual countries have shifted, as priorities change and as progress is made towards particular objectives. This is as it should be; the area is a dynamic one and policies and definitions need to remain relevant. In the context of the OECD E-Government Project, the term "e-government" is defined as:

OECD Definition of E-Government

**The use of information and communication technologies,
and particularly the Internet, as a tool to achieve better government.**

While the relative importance of the Internet in the overall framework of ICT use in government will be a matter for debate for a long time to come, this report focuses more on use of ICT that involves the Internet than other, more established ICT applications. This is in recognition of the fact that use of the Internet is in its relative infancy, and as such raises more issues for public administrators and governments generally than the use of more established technologies. The Internet, building on the established base of ICT use by governments, offers new opportunities for governments to do their job better, and it is primarily for this reason that governments are focusing on it. However, e-government is more than Internet use or online service delivery. Internet use by governments cannot, and indeed should not, be isolated from the broader digitisation of government activity as a whole; the issue is therefore one of emphasis.

1.3. Objectives

As will become clear in the course of this report, it is well recognised that changes involving ICTs need to be accompanied by broader organisational change if they are to be effective. Merely introducing ICTs into existing organisations and work processes will not produce the desired improved outcomes. This report aims to identify what needs to change if e-government benefits are to be maximised. It is designed to assist e-government practitioners and those concerned with the modernisation and reform of public administrations. It analyses country experiences and good practices, identifies key challenges and impacts, and sets down possible strategies and guidelines as a framework for action by individual countries. There is no single path to good governance outcomes via e-government, and each country's action will reflect its individual governance and economic and social circumstances and priorities.

The OECD Project's priorities were to analyse e-government within the framework of public governance, so this report does not evaluate countries' e-government activity, nor does it attempt to rank or undertake a comparative analysis of progress in advancing e-government objectives. A number of organisations have undertaken statistical analysis of e-government initiatives, and some of this analysis is included in Annex 2. However, countries participating in the OECD study are sceptical about existing statistical studies, as they give only a superficial picture of e-government and do not usually take into account country priorities, service quality, or any of the back-office changes that this report argues are essential for e-government. Moreover, existing data cannot measure the degree of co-operation between services nor the quality of user friendliness – two essential aspects of this study. The OECD is currently laying the groundwork for further analysis of these issues, including eventual quantitative evaluations (see the section on Monitoring and Evaluation).

Instead, this report seeks to be **forward looking** and to consider the longer-term vision by addressing the following questions:

● Where are we now, and where are we going?

- How can governments meet future challenges?
- What are the pathways to the longer-term vision?

More specifically, for the purposes of this report, the **full range of government public administration activity** is addressed – planning and policy making, service delivery, e-consultation and internal management. Particular attention is paid to experiences at national government level, although relations between national and other levels of government are examined insofar as the latter are partners in meeting national policy objectives.

The study **focuses on governance issues and impacts**. E-government can help administrations do their job better by reinforcing good governance objectives and administrative reforms are necessary if e-government is to be successful. E-government and reform are therefore mutually reinforcing. This study takes the perspective that the value of e-government initiatives can be assessed against long-standing governance principles, such as efficiency and accountability. It recognises that introducing e-government initiatives will challenge existing governance frameworks, such as those dealing with how public administrations operate, and considers potential solutions.

1.4. Methodology

The findings and observations presented in this study emerge from the deliberations and guidance of the OECD E-Government Working Group. This group consisted of 12 countries: Australia, Canada, Denmark, Finland, France, Germany, Italy, Japan, Korea, Mexico, Netherlands and the United States. The findings of the report also stem from the series of Project seminars, involving commissioned papers and the seminar deliberations; from papers and information prepared by member countries; and from analysis of countries' e-government strategies and other material. As will appear, there are major deficiencies in data on e-government activities, so that it has been impossible to carry out a detailed analysis of comparable quantitative information.

The examples and information used in this text come largely from the OECD E-Government Working Group. The OECD also undertook an in-depth pilot study of e-government in Finland, and many examples and case studies stem from the report of that study, "E-Government in Finland". Country examples in the report are taken from all levels of government.

ISBN 92-64-10117-9
The E-Government Imperative
© OECD 2003

Chapter 2

The Case for E-Government

Public management reforms to enhance performance continue to be an important issue for all OECD governments. The need to respond to changing pressures resulting from globalisation, fiscal demands, evolving societies and customer expectations has meant a continuing process of reform, notwithstanding significant changes over the last two decades. While common elements can be identified, particularly the need to do more with less, the timing, pace and nature of reforms have been diverse, reflecting the conditions for reform and the strategies adopted in each country.

Reforms have addressed the full range of good governance objectives, seeking legitimacy, rule of law, transparency, accountability, integrity, effectiveness, coherence, adaptability, participation and consultation. In many areas, ICTs have been an important enabling tool for reform. While the pursuit of efficiency gains and the effective delivery of programme outcomes have been main drivers of ICT use in government, the focus has turned more recently to other good governance objectives, such as improving services, increasing accountability and transparency and facilitating consultation and engagement.

This Chapter looks at the reasons for embracing e-government as a means of reforming public management and contributing to broader policy objectives. In practice, while a specific e-government initiative can be driven by a single major goal, such as cost savings, most aim to achieve a number of often competing objectives. Drawing on information submitted by Working Group members, this Chapter discusses the case for e-government:

- **E-government helps improve efficiency in government.** ICTs are a necessary enabler of reforms to the ways in which public administrations work. Improving internal operating systems – financial systems, purchasing and payment arrangements, internal communications and sharing of information – and programme processing and delivery arrangements can generate operating efficiencies and improve performance.

- **Enhanced quality of service** has been a major component of public administration reform over the past two decades, and the use of ICTs to generate improvements in services has been a primary driver for e-government activity. In particular, the use of the Internet has given a major boost to customer-focused, seamless services, which aim to transcend the structure of public administrations. Online services are increasingly seen as part of a broader services strategy, with important customer and efficiency benefits. As users of public services are often obliged to interact with government, user dissatisfaction with the quality of government services can quickly become a major political issue.

- ICTs can support **more effective outcomes** in key policy areas such as health, welfare services, security and education. Ultimately, governments and public administrations exist to deliver policy outcomes, and ICTs are a major enabler across all major policy areas. The use of the Internet to deliver value in these areas is a major preoccupation in member countries.

- Better governance arrangements in themselves will **promote economic policy objectives**. More specific effects may range from impacts on ICT production, e-commerce diffusion and business productivity to indirect effects such as reduced fiscal requirements owing to more effective programmes and efficiencies flowing through to the broader economy.

- E-government can help **forward the reform agenda**. When aligned with modernisation goals, implementing e-government can help administrations focus on the additional changes needed to meet service delivery and good governance concerns. At the same time, it provides some valuable reform tools and builds support from high-level leaders and government employees for achieving those objectives.

- Through citizen engagement, e-government can **improve the overall trust relationship** between government and public administrations. E-government, by improving information flows and encouraging active participation by citizens is increasingly seen as a valuable tool for building trust between governments and citizens.

These objectives may involve trade-offs between efficiency and effectiveness, efficiency and openness, accountability and customer focus. When this is the case, priorities will need to be set, but it should not be assumed that such trade-offs are inevitable. Several Nordic countries have put in place specific offices (ombudsmen) to handle citizen complains with regard to privacy and citizen trust, this supports both privacy protection and efficient use of data.

2.1. E-government and efficiency

The search for **efficiency gains** is a major driver of ICT use in government, and most national strategies specifically address this goal. ICT use in government has often been driven by the need to reduce the call on resources, either to reduce overall spending or to allocate funds to higher priority areas. Mass processing tasks, distributed networks of service outlets, payment processes and internal public administration operating processes such as procurement, payroll and human resource management all depend on ICTs to operate and will continue to be targets for efficiencies.

Box 1. Italy: Transforming the relationship with business suppliers to government

In order to increase programme efficiency, effectiveness and to stimulate e-commerce, in 2000, the Ministry of Economy and Finance adopted an e-procurement system. This was the result of a study which identified areas in which procurement processes could be made more efficient. It reflected one of the goals of the Italian E-government Action Plan to improve economic development, promote change and modernisation in the public administration and develop the Information Society.

In the new e-procurement system, the approach to procurement has been transformed, and ICT applications and re-engineered business processes have been introduced. Three procurement channels or "platforms" have been introduced: online product catalogues, e-auctions and e-marketplaces.

In order to introduce the new procedures, new legislation had to be introduced to provide a legal basis for the e-procurement project. Based on this, a new organisational model for procurement management and a new online website were introduced. While reforming and centralising policies and procedures, care was taken to respect the budget autonomy of agencies – purchasing decisions remain within the authority of the respective agencies, while the e-procurement system simply enables a more effective process for the authority to be exercised. A new online procurement website was also introduced, based on the platform model, which provides a fully transactional and e-enabled capacity that allows bids and purchases to be made online.

The e-procurement system has meant a 30% reduction in the total cost of goods and services procured for the government. The end-to-end transactional capacity has meant that suppliers wanting to secure government business have had to adopt e-commerce business practices, and the increasing use of e-procurement will eventually provide further business opportunities, such as collaboration with suppliers on inventory requirements and new applications to automate purchasing.

Source: Culbertson (2002b).

More recently, Internet-based applications have been deployed, using online filing to cut down costs of data re-entry and checking, to save on communications costs with customers and within government, to use scarce resources such as skilled staff or facilities more efficiently by improving booking arrangements, to replace paper-based application processes and to reform payment and procurement.

385424

EXTENZA - TURPIN

Blackhorse Road Letchworth Herts SG6 1HN

Your order has been packed with care to ensure that all items are received in the same condition that they left our warehouse.

We also believe that your order has been processed in an efficient manner.

If for any reason you are not satisfied please return this slip to our Customer Services Department quoting your customer and invoice numbers shown on the despatch documentation which accompanied this parcel. They will deal with any queries immediately.

THANK YOU FOR ORDERING THROUGH EXTENZA - TURPIN

Customer Service Telephone: +44(0)1462 672555

Extenza-Turpin is a trading name of Turpin Distribution Services Limited

Box 2. **Improved efficiency in statistical offices**

One example of improved efficiency as a result of e-government can be seen in international and national statistical institutions.

Changes have occurred in national statistical offices (NSOs) in response to growing citizen demand for more statistical data, disseminated on a more cost-effective basis, in order to take decisions or evaluate the performance of governments. The developments have been made possible by recent technological advances in ICT. Changes in work practices have been so fundamental that NSOs are usually to the fore of the e-government process in their countries in providing information, interactive services for data manipulation or information sharing with other agencies.

Advanced technology, and the Internet in particular, has enabled national statistical authorities to disseminate data more rapidly, and more cost-effectively. It has provided new opportunities to create national knowledge bases by placing large data bases on the Internet, as well as to create and manage very large databases. These databases are accessible through the Internet and allow products to be tailored to individual users which are updated in real time. Many governments have also developed national one-stop statistical portals, which offer statistical information to users without them having to know the agency that produced them, providing integrated information across administrative boundaries. They often operate within the framework of a wider government portal.

National statistical offices also use ICT to use the expanding range of statistical tools to elaborate elementary data and to make ready-to-use products available to clients, to respond to the requirements of international bodies and comply with international standards regarding both data and metadata, and to disseminate more data free of charge in recognition that official statistics can often be a key public good. Due to ICT, as well as a commitment to change, many statistical offices are now using data sourced from administrative records instead of direct collection. This reduces the compliance burden on citizens and businesses, and has achieved budget savings. ICT has also enabled NSOs to use different variations of legal, administrative, methodological and technical measures to collect and disseminate data in a way that protects the privacy of respondents by preventing primary and secondary disclosure. It also provides efficiency gains when disseminating data that may require enhanced security measures. While there is no such thing as zero-risk of disclosure, NSOs are now able to minimise this risk while at the same time making better quality data available.

Statistical offices are using ICT advances to make efficiency gains in the area of public service delivery for which they are responsible, *i.e.* the collection, compilation and dissemination of statistics. But success has been achieved as much due to issues such as leadership, commitment, planning, and involvement of many different actors as to the use of ICT.

Source: Finn and E. Giovannini (2002).

> ## Box 3. The Nordic "Green Corridor" – international data sharing for increased efficiency
>
> An example of increased efficiency is the Nordic "Green Corridor" system, in which electronic sharing of information has helped customs officials manage processes with greater speed and at reduced cost. In co-operation with Swedish trade, Finnish customs, Finnish trade and Russian customs, Swedish customs have developed a system to facilitate border crossing when entering Russia for compliant operators. The Green Corridor is based on the accreditation of customs processes and a fully electronic chain of information, starting with the Swedish or Finnish trader and ending with the Russian customs officers at the point of entry. Via the Internet, Russian customs has access to the trader's customs declaration submitted online and thus can better plan and perform control measures. This makes mutual risk analyses possible and ensures that control measures are performed only when high risk is perceived.
>
> An approved Swedish or Finnish trader joining the Green Corridor enjoys a release time of a maximum of two hours when entering Russian territory, since all necessary information is already available when the merchandise appears at the border. Special measures ensure the authenticity of submitted information and electronic signatures guarantee consistency from consignor to consignee.
>
> The Green Corridor promotes compliance on the international level and makes use of the e-solutions implemented within the Virtual Customs Office of Swedish Customs. True partnership applies since the services of the Virtual Customs Office are also available to approved traders in Finland and the information submitted is available for the three customs administrations in Sweden, Finland and Russia.
>
> *Source:* OECD E-Government Working Group.

With the increasing introduction of seamless online government services, significant future efficiencies are likely as a result of greater sharing of data within government and between government and private sectors such as health care and welfare services. Arrangements which allow for re-use of data (ignoring for the moment service quality and greater effectiveness) can create efficiencies by reducing the need for multiple collections from the same customer, data reconciliation and checking, and indeed, from the point of view of the customer, for the need for some services at all. If progress is to be made, the key issues are privacy protection and the need for agencies to operate in a common framework to enable interoperability.

Additionally, major savings can be obtained by transforming business processes. More recently, the focus has turned to the Internet and online applications in areas such as online data collection to reduce data entry costs, the use of e-procurement and other e-commerce applications, reductions in government publication and distribution costs and data through online publication. Sharing of common data within and between agencies to reduce collection and data reconciliation costs is emerging as a major focus of efforts to reduce costs within government. It also provides considerable benefit to customers of government services.

It is generally thought that greater efficiencies are generated from ICT projects that involve a major transformation of business process than from those that do not. While this is broadly true, the cumulative contribution of **micro-efficiencies** should not be ignored, even though the absolute amounts involved may not be significant.

While improvements in efficiency are a major factor in the decision to implement e-government programmes, a focus on efficiency through the use of ICT requires consideration of the following:

● Assessments of efficiency in government are difficult. **Government outputs are difficult to quantify**; as with other service industries increases in quality

---

Box 4. Germany: Online services and the Federal Education Assistance Act (BAFög)

BAFög is aimed at promoting schooling and higher education. It enables children of low-income families to finance their education through a loan. Beneficiaries have to repay their loans upon completion of their studies. Currently, some EUR 650 million are provided annually in the form of loans for the education of school and university students. For the first time, students repaying their BAFög loans are given the opportunity to obtain information on their applications, questions and requests over the Internet. This includes early repayments, performance-related partial remission of debts as well as release from or deferment of loan repayment. Using BaFög online, beneficiaries can apply online for performance-related or social reductions before paying off their loans.

The aim is to develop co-operation between the federal, Länder (federal states) and municipality levels on BaFög matters, and to further standardise relevant management processes. The electronic processing of repayments has already led to savings of EUR 4.5 million in the first year of operations. These savings are primarily due to process optimisation efforts, and investments in this e-government service paid for themselves in less than one year. Further savings can be achieved across the various administrative levels.

Source: OECD E-Government Working Group.

---

are difficult to measure; the political satisfaction of particular projects or policies may legitimately outweigh more mundane considerations of cost and savings

- These concerns apply to the assessment of efficiency gains as a result of e-government, as do issues around assessing the impacts of ICT use more generally. At the individual project level assessments of potential efficiencies are often made at the project initiation stage, although it is not uncommon in government for an ICT enabled process to be introduced within tight time lines to meet a specific policy and political imperative, with efficiency concerns of lesser importance. However, while individual project-level efficiencies can be identified, at the aggregate level the **lack of an accepted methodology and comparable data** make it difficult to draw conclusions as to the scale of the aggregate impact of e-government on efficiency.

- Notwithstanding these problems, at the project level efficiencies need to be able to be identified and estimated prior to the endorsement of the project, to enable the assessment of competing proposals. As part of this, the **need** for the particular service or process should be examined. Invariably such assessments are made within an agency, but should take place on a whole of government basis. It may be possible for an agency to remove the need for users of a service to contact government by re-using data already collected by a different agency, or to build on existing processes.

2.2. E-government improves service quality

The improvement of government services is an objective of all e-government policy statements examined in this study. Indeed, given the emphasis in both policies and in commentary more generally on online service issues and online service targets, one might assume this to be the sole objective of e-government. It has been useful as a way of raising public interest in e-government, by articulating a vision (for example, services online by a specific date) often with the broader aim of engagement with information society initiatives more generally. Online service targets have also been effective in mobilising public administrations to examine the potential of the Internet and related technologies by applying them to existing services.

Specific service delivery policies have been developed by governments to improve the quality of their services to customers. Key elements here have comprised quality charters, incorporating timelines for specific services, agency/customer service standards, benchmarking with private sector service organisations and customer surveys. While a certain desire can exist to have online services for their own sake or for their demonstration effect, such services are increasingly being developed in the context of broader, multi-channel service policies.

THE E-GOVERNMENT IMPERATIVE – ISBN 92-64-10117-9 – © OECD 2003

A core element of member countries' reform agendas and e-government strategies is the adoption of a **customer focus**, with the specific objective of providing citizens and businesses with a coherent interface with government which reflects their needs rather than the structure of government. This customer focus has long been an element of broader public management reform, and predates the generalised use of the Internet as a service delivery mechanism. One-stop offices, advice bureaux, whole of government telephone call centres and services such as information kiosks have attempted to bring together information and services from different governmental agencies. The provision of case management services, drawing together a range of programme resources to address individual needs also reflects this approach.

The availability of the Internet has lead to a quantum leap in efforts to provide a cross-government customer focus, and Member countries are active in developing initiatives that draw together information and services for specific customer groups. Citizens benefit from online services because they can learn about policy changes that may affect them or specific community activities or proposals at local level and can carry out routine transactions with government, such as payments, on a more convenient basis.

From the point of view of users, ICTs have made it easier to integrate the services of individual agencies. To date, this has overwhelmingly concerned Web-based information services, such as overall government portals and sub-portals focused on a particular subject or customer group. Such services require co-ordinated activity across agencies, with agreement on standards for metadata, for example. Integrated cross-agency transaction services are starting to emerge, and are under active consideration in many member countries.

Specific online initiatives adopted to improve customer focus include:

- Development of **online portals** focused on particular topics or groups which bring together information and transactions relating to that particular topic or group.

- Measures that provide **targeting** within customer groupings, such as the ability to select information by size of business from a business portal, which helps small businesses find relevant information more readily, or access to information by geographical area.

- Use of **e-mail listings** to provide information, for example release by national statistical agencies of new statistical information customised for specific groups of customers.

- Services that allow individual **identified users** to access customised information and services. This could involve, for example, access to targeted information and capacity to submit taxation or other forms, to apply for assistance and to file compliance-returns online. Such services

Box 5. Canada: Guide for the Service Improvement Initiative

This guide is a managerial tool for implementing the Service Improvement Initiative. It is directed to programme managers responsible for service delivery in federal departments and agencies. It offers a detailed, holistic method for planning and implementing service improvement, based on the client's perspective and the establishment of service standards. It includes step-by-step descriptions of suggested activities with associated evaluation tools, questionnaires and guidelines in the appendices.

Source: Service Improvement Initiative: *www.cio-dpi.gc.ca/si-as/howto-comment/hotwo-comment00_e.asp*

require some form of authentication related to the confidentiality and security requirements of the transaction involved. Many countries have realised the benefits of cross-agency authentication systems, and the United Kingdom's Gateway and Ireland's Vault projects aim to provide a common authentication point for a range of services. They also provide an important enabler for online mass customisation of services.

Box 6. Mexico: Customer-focused portals

The Government of Mexico recently launched *www.gob.mx*, a government-wide portal that organizes information and services in a thematic, rather than institutional, fashion. The system concentrates more than 1 500 informative and transactional services from over a hundred government institutions. Under the theme "work", for example, users will not only find the expected matchmaker service between employers and prospective recruits, but also information about labour rights, taxation on labour services, public housing and soft financing for low income workers, and so on. Furthermore, contents are linked among themselves to produce contextual connections such as "youth" and "drug prevention", or "household" and "security". The bundling of information and services in thematic channels has been possible thanks to the horizontal coordination of sixteen leaders – one for each thematic channel – and the work of several dozen agencies.

Source: OECD E-Government Working Group.

2.3. E-government increases policy effectiveness

Although access and convenience are important drivers of much e-government activity, there is increasing awareness that e-government initiatives can also help achieve important outcomes in major policy areas such as health, education, anti-crime initiatives and security. In fact, efforts to improve enhanced policy outcomes will encompass the full range of the policy sectors addressed by governments. The contribution of e-government to policy outcomes may take many forms, but a characteristic of effective initiatives is the use of the networking potential of the Internet to share data more effectively among a range of dispersed stakeholders.

E-government initiatives may involve online services that interact directly with end users, for example to provide information and enrolment facilities to boost take-up of a welfare payment programme or online information on education and training options. Initiatives may also involve sharing information among various units of governments and intermediaries, for example in the health sector, where arrangements are made to capture and share more efficiently information on pharmaceutical use and medical services in order to reduce aggregate costs and provide better care to individuals. Such initiatives are being developed in countries such as Finland and Australia.

Improved collection of taxes, reduced demand for health services through better use of health information or reduced unemployment payments owing to better matching of the unemployed to vacancies via online job registers can also have a significant impact on government's fiscal position.

Additionally, e-government can help improve social policy. For example, e-government can help administrations promote the use of native languages and provide information about indigenous peoples. It can help form communities of interest around public issues and provide information to specific and disenfranchised groups.

An increase in programme effectiveness through the use of ICT will require attention to the following:

- A framework for identifying and assessing the potential contribution to the relevant policy target. Many e-government initiatives have been developed from a supply-side "build and they will come" focus. While this is understandable in the early stages of online service rollout, initiatives need to meet a clear business need if they are to be effective. There is a need to be able to measure potential demand, policy outcomes and quality improvements that can result from e-government initiatives.

- Recognition of the fact that capturing the benefits of better information flows and networking in general is complex in sectors such as health and

Box 7. **Denmark: User benefits expected from health portal**

A collaborative effort to establish a common public health portal on the Internet is a fundamental element of the introduction of digital administration in Denmark. Based upon the initiative of the Danish regions, the health portal initiative became a part of the 2002 economic agreement between the government, the regions and certain local authorities and stressed the project's importance as a framework for electronic communication in the area of healthcare. Phase one of the portal is expected to be launched at the end of 2003 and run through 2004.

The health portal's overall purpose is to support the general aims of Danish National Health Service (NHS), including better information and service, quality assurance and improved use of treatment and care resources. It is intended to give targeted access to the NHS, affording users opportunities for information and communication in order to gain insight when necessary into their possibilities for treatment. At the same time, the principle that healthcare problems must as far as possible be solved at the primary treatment level (typically general practitioners – GPs) must be respected.

As a means of facilitating communication between the parties involved in the NHS, it is crucial for the health portal to be seen as a tool capable of being integrated into clinical work in such a manner as to allow healthcare professionals to solve the tasks supported by the portal in a quicker and/or better way.

Security is the first concern for the health portal. Patients may only access their own data following individual authentication via digital signature. Healthcare professionals may access patient data after obtaining the relevant consent and local authentication.

The search engine is expected to be the most frequently used access mode. The quality of search results for the large amounts of varied data that the portal will contain will be highly dependent on the accessibility and quality of metadata. Automatic generation of metadata and use of classifications that match the NHS's usage are therefore essential.

The portal must support a coherent patient treatment process, including supporting patient opportunities for attending to their own healthcare and their own treatment and for contacting relevant healthcare professionals, and supporting transfer procedures between healthcare professionals involved in the treatment process. Support of patients with chronic illness through home monitoring and telemedicine is envisaged.

To avoid duplication, the portal where possible use information produced under the auspices of the public healthcare authorities. This principle will be reinforced through the establishment of a central editing function and through regional editing environments. The editors will be responsible for further developing and updating a range of information, including profile areas for NHS actors, national waiting list information, patient guidelines, information on healthcare and prevention, etc.

Box 7.   **Denmark: User benefits expected from health portal**
(*cont.*)

During the first two years, selected counties' electronic patient medical records are to be integrated. In addition, to ensure more appropriate use of medicines and remedy inappropriate polypharmacy, personal medical profiles will contain a review of the use of prescription medicines. This information will be adapted and used for communication between health-care professionals.

Patients will also be able to communicate with their GPs through electronic appointments, e-mail consultations and ordering of repeat prescriptions. There will also be a pilot project on GPs' receipt of test results from medical laboratories. The health portal will also support communication between general practitioners and hospitals concerning examination information, clinical guidelines, etc.

Source: Denmark Country Paper (2002).

welfare services and will require both patience and full engagement by stakeholders. Timeframes must be realistic, and there may be considerable lags before benefits accrue.

● Sharing of information about individuals between different units of government and between governments and non-government organisations and enterprises raises issues of privacy protection. The need to justify such sharing reinforces the need to articulate clearly the benefits to be reaped.

2.4. E-government contributes to economic policy objectives

The New Economy: Beyond the Hype (OECD, 2001f) assessed the impact of ICTs on economic growth and indicated that assessment is difficult in this area, particularly for activities within the government sphere. E-government activity may generate savings for governments by reducing the need for outlays, but the economic impact will depend on how these savings are used. Accordingly, no firm conclusions as to the scale of aggregate impacts can be drawn; moreover, as will be seen, assessment of impacts at the specific project level presents significant difficulties.

Online services have already played a strong role in **improving business productivity** and assisting in the start-up of new enterprises. In many OECD countries, administrative simplification is a priority, especially as regards policies and services for small businesses, as government requirements can have a major impact on their viability. Initiatives have involved reducing compliance burdens by making business registration requirements accessible

> ### Box 8. Spain: The tourism portal: a market place for tourist products and services
>
> Developed by the government and launched in June 2002, the Spanish tourism portal *www.spain.info* aggregates information and services from public and private sector databases (*i.e.* the central government, the 17 regional autonomous administrations, local authorities, private tour operators, travel agents, individual hotels, restaurants, etc.). It shares information and services with vertical and horizontal portals, such as municipal websites, commercial portals, travel sites and government tourist offices. The portal provides tourists and travel agents with quantified and co-ordinated information to plan, organise and book trips in nine languages and a wide range of formats (*e.g.* multimedia and 3-D virtual imagery), and allows tourist office staff to deliver up-to-date information tailored to each tourist's needs. The portal allows regions, municipalities and private operators to pursue their own tourism strategy without having to duplicate efforts. An e-commerce extranet allows tourism businesses and communities to buy and sell their products, and provides a reservation system, with financial transactions conducted at the point of sale.
>
> *Source:* Holmes (2002b).

online, enabling online filing of taxation forms directly from accounting software used by businesses. They also concern providing online access or filing of forms relating to unemployment insurance or statistical reporting and sharing data collected from businesses among different agencies. Governments have also developed online business portals to provide more efficient access to information produced by business assistance agencies on issues such as market trends, export opportunities and assistance programmes. Portals have been used to draw together information from a range of agencies, often at different levels of government.

E-government is also seen as a means of promoting broader **information society and e-commerce policies.** Government use of online applications for service delivery and government business processes can provide a demonstration effect which can help lead to the take-up of e-commerce and the Internet across the economy more broadly. This is a common goal of countries' information society and e-government strategies, though its success remains difficult to assess. Elements of this policy may include:

- Government acting as a **leading-edge user**, adopting emerging applications to assist in their broader take-up across the economy. For example, governments have been urged to adopt smart card or specific security applications in the hopes that this will provide a critical mass for broader use. In a context of promoting innovation, these approaches can be worthwhile, particularly if specific funding is forthcoming.

- Developing or adopting **policies and standards** which can be applied across government and broader public sector applications, in order to promote common standards and influence the potential market. Sweden and Australia, for example, have adopted policies to share authentication infrastructure between government and the banking sector to defray costs and promote take up, and thus improve the business situation for both parties.

- E-government services can be seen as a rationale for **take up of the Internet,** thus contributing not just to social policy objectives to reduce the digital divide but also, more broadly, to the value of online access in the community (the network effect) and thus to the demand for online services and e-commerce.

- Government **direct consumption of ICT goods and services** can be significant and is often more stable than private-sector demand. Government demand for communications capacity, particularly in non-metropolitan areas, can influence market decisions to roll out capacity. Additionally, government demand for ICT can increase demand for locally produced ICT products and services, and government ICT procurement policies often take into account this objective. Governments can also help develop ICT skills in the economy.

2.5. E-government can help forward the public reform agenda

The promised benefits of e-governments do not take place simply by digitising information and placing it online. E-government services continue to be embedded in the environment of today's public administrations and therefore remain limited by what these administrations are capable, and willing, to do. The term "e-government", as used by the OECD E-Government Project, applies to the use of ICT as a tool to *achieve better government*. Thus, e-government is not about business as usual, but should instead focus on using ICT to transform the structures, operations and, most importantly, the culture of government.

Reform of the public administration has been on the agendas of most OECD governments well before the advent of the term "e-government". But e-government is an important component of today's reform agendas because it: 1) serves as a tool for reform; 2) renews interest in public management reform; 3) highlights internal inconsistencies; 4) underscores commitment to good governance objectives.

As a reform tool, ICT use in government makes it easier to monitor the efficiency and effectiveness of service delivery, tying individual output to overall project objectives. It has been used to simplify and make more transparent financial, case management and human resource management processes. Such tools are only effective, however, if they are linked to public management objectives and used as part of an overall change management strategy.

E-mail and electronic communications technologies have laid the groundwork for the much heralded "webbed" or non-hierarchical administration by allowing collaborative editing of documents, broader sharing of information and the tracking of documents waiting for clearance. One of the most important implications for e-government is its potential for integrating services and processes in order to achieve more seamless government. Seamless government cuts across the boundaries that separate different jobs or functions in the public administration. E-government can create networks of information flow among the different parts of the administration, irrespective of legislative or administrative boundaries and/or hierarchies. In fact, one can question whether or not government agencies can maintain their current internal divisions and territories while trying to maintain a single, simple interface with the citizen through e-government.

E-government has also helped to renew interest in public management reform by capturing the imagination of political leaders and government employees alike. While there is a danger of overselling the benefits of e-government, there is interest in both the potential for service improvements and the participatory aspects of e-government. Public sector trade unions in many countries have been supportive of e-government initiatives. Especially in the context of shrinking working populations, e-government may offer more skilled employment for some even as some less-skilled jobs are eliminated. Government interest in ICT has also renewed focus on developing employee skills and on recruitment and retention.

E-government also increases pressure for reform by promising service improvements. Once countries begin implementation, they realise that technology alone is insufficient and that workplace practices and structures need to be reformed as well. E-government raises citizen expectations putting further pressure on government. For example, Statskontoret, the Swedish Agency for Administrative Development, notes that serving citizens 24 hours a day, seven days a week is not simply about having a web presence: "the 24/7 agency, must, through its choice and implementation of service channels and electronic services, become part of the larger context that is central e-government. This calls for voluntary collaboration between agencies or government-led development and strategy throughout the central public administration." (The 24/7 Agency. Statskontoret, 2000.)

> ### Box 9. **Switzerland: "Live+" – Internet transmission of parliamentary debates**
>
> Live+ transmits the live debates of the National Council (lower house) and the Council of States (upper house) of the United Federal Assembly (the Swiss Parliament), along with supplementary information to put the debates into context. Web users follow debates live in one window of their computer screen and, on a second and third window, interactively call up information about the speaker and the issue being debated. It is up to viewers to decide how deeply they would like to investigate a particular subject.
>
> Live+ is an audiovisual Internet relay system, produced by the Swiss Parliamentary Services in conjunction with Swiss Television. It was launched in 1999 as a result of demands for greater transparency in the work of both houses of Parliament from citizens, the media and cantonal authorities who increasingly wanted to follow the debates. Live+ makes the debates accessible to a wider audience than television. For instance, Swiss embassies and citizens living abroad can now follow the debates live. From the same website, users can also call other parliamentary information, such as the schedule of sessions, the Official Bulletin of the Federal Assembly, and data relating to committee work.
>
> Parliament's website: *www.parlament.ch*
>
> Source: Holmes (2002b).

Finally, e-government raises good governance issues that are at the heart of many current debates on how to improve relations between government and citizens. As noted by the OECD Ministerial Council (2001), good governance is an essential ingredient of the mix of policies that underpin economic growth and development. By contributing to reduced corruption, greater openness and trust in government institutions, e-government can help to meet economic policy objectives and build citizen trust in government.

Much has been made about the potential for new technologies to increase the transparency and accountability of government. One cannot assume, however, that making services available online will automatically increase the transparency of the public administration. Undeniably, the enhanced information dissemination capacity of the Internet increases the pressure on government to be more transparent. But it is up to governments to decide, in dialogue with citizens, business and civil society, how best to safeguard the public interest, reconciling the search for better knowledge management with the demand for data privacy and responding to pressures for greater transparency and disclosure at reasonable cost.

It is worth keeping in mind the incentives, opportunities and constraints of the public administrations that are being asked to carry out e-government initiatives. In the wake of the events of 11 September 2001, for example, legitimate policy objectives of security have, in many instances superseded concerns about transparency. The question is not whether one is more important than the other, but rather have countries laid out the appropriate criteria for deciding among diverse governance concerns?

Modernising government structures and processes to meet e-government demands will have some fundamental impacts on how services are delivered. The current model of the public administration in most OECD countries, for example, restricts information sharing because the collection and use of data is segmented along with the structure of government. This separation according to functions, however, also serves to protect privacy of citizens' data. In creating a more seamless government, government will have to strike an equilibrium between protecting citizens' privacy and better meeting their

---

Box 10. United Kingdom: Engaging the citizen in a "new" government – The Scottish Parliament

Since 2000, the Scottish Parliament has committed to using ICTS to advance its principles of openness, accountability and citizen engagement in the parliamentary process, and implemented an innovative e-government strategy to engage the citizen and assist the operations of the new parliament and the government administration.

The use of the web by the Scottish Parliament *www.scottish.parliament.uk* is an innovative and evolving model for how ICTs can be used to inform and engage citizens in the democratic process, with an open approach to information and reporting on parliamentary processes, which helps to strengthen the transparency and accountability of parliament to citizens. It includes public education about Parliament's functions and mandate. It uses web casting to broadcast parliamentary session and committee meetings. Parliament also uses ICT to better engage citizens directly in the democratic process, by enabling citizens to petition parliament online. The website contains extensive material and resources on petitioning, including: how to petition, a registry of petitions, and actions taken. Direct citizen participation is also encouraged through interactive "Discussion Boards" on the website. Other web-based resources enable citizens to contact their Members of Scottish Parliament (MSP), and lists the portfolios and committees in which the MSP serves and links to them.

Source: Culbertson (2002b).

---

needs with more efficient, pro-active services. What starts as an exercise aimed at developing more responsive programs and services becomes an exercise in governance (Lenihan 2002).

2.6. Citizen engagement and trust

Citizen engagement can help build and strengthen the trust relationship between governments and citizens. This is fundamental to the achievement of good governance and in turn to fulfilling broader economic and social goals. In the absence of trust, the rule of law, the legitimacy of government decisions and specific reform agendas may be called into question. While the overall relationship involves a complex web of factors, ICTs can act as an enabler to engage citizens in the policy process, promote open and accountable government and help prevent corruption. Citizen engagement at a basic level includes information, consultation and feedback by service users. At a more advanced level it includes citizen engagement for policy making.

Access to information, consultation and participation mechanisms can have a pervasive impact on promotion of good governance. In themselves, they identify a willingness by governments and administrations to not only accept public scrutiny and accountability, but to actively facilitate it, by improving the scope and efficiency of these processes. This makes good sense: opening up decision-making processes can improve the quality of decisions by improving decision makers' understanding of the context and impact of options before them.

The nature of online services facilitates the collection of information on user experiences. At one level, data on Web use can provide information on pages accessed, user pathways through information and points where users abandoned the application. More active feedback from short online questionnaires or feedback contacts, while not representative, can provide qualitative information directly based on user experiences. Fine-tuning the presentation of online information can reduce the number of costly follow-up contacts, for example if applications are not filled in correctly. Transactions that can be completed online effectively can generate considerable savings.

Feedback from users can help refine service arrangements to make them more effective. For example user feedback on the design of forms or the way information is presented can help ensure that citizens are aware of entitlements and requirements.

Opening up decision-making processes can improve the quality of decisions by enriching decision makers' understanding of the context and impact of the options before them. Consultation and informed participation can help lead to policies that better address constituents' needs and also increase support for, and trust in, public institutions and their policies.

Governments are actively developing online applications in these areas, and many countries are also developing e-democracy policies, which may include e-voting and political engagement issues.

However, while new ICTs offer significant opportunities for greater stakeholder engagement in policy making, they also raise a host of new questions for government. How are citizens' rights of access to information to be ensured in the online era? What aspects of government's current structure, organisation and resource allocation need to change to respond to new standards for their interactions with citizens? What is the status of civil servants' online responses to citizens' queries or their submissions to an electronic discussion forum?

Box 11. Korea: Improving transparency by building an electronic procurement system

In the past, suppliers for government procurement projects obtained bid information through personal networks and placed bids that were prearranged by the supplier and procuring organisation. In addition, this involved many visits to the procuring organisation to receive payment. This kind of interaction, which depended on direct contact between the supplying firm and procuring public entity, always meant the possibility of corruption.

System G2B (Government to Business) makes possible total online processing of government procurement, from placing bids to final payment. The procurement portal gives access to procurement information in one stroke (*www.g2b.go.kr*). Through the use of this system, direct contact to place bids and receive payment has been drastically reduced and the procurement process has been disclosed to the public, thereby improving transparency and the credibility of procurement practices.

Source: OECD E-Government Working Group.

Box 12. Mexico: Preventing corruption in procurement

The site *www.compranet.gob.mx* was created to handle all purchases by the federal government and has expanded to include states and some cities. The system has been crucial for ensuring the transparency of the government's procurement process. It includes capabilities for electronic tendering, special searches, and research on both vendors and buyers. Citizens can readily find out who has bought what, from whom and at what price.

Source: OECD E-Government Working Group.

THE E-GOVERNMENT IMPERATIVE – ISBN 92-64-10117-9 – © OECD 2003

ISBN 92-64-10117-9
The E-Government Imperative
© OECD 2003

Chapter 3

External Barriers to E-Government

Identifying potential gains from e-government is one thing; actually realising them is another. Implementing ICT projects, particularly large-scale projects that can have a major impact on service quality improvements or efficiencies, can raise a number of problems, many of which relate particularly to operating within government. External e-government barriers often concern breakdowns, missing components or lack of flexibility in the government-wide frameworks that enable e-government. The result is oftentimes the inability to achieve a whole-of-government perspective in e-government implementation. Legislative and regulatory barriers, financial barriers, technological barriers and the digital divide, among others, can impede the uptake of e-government. While internal obstacles (such as lack of collaboration for seamless services) will be covered in the chapter on Implementation, these external barriers need to be addressed on a whole of government basis in order to be overcome.

3.1. Legislative and regulatory barriers

The success of e-government initiatives and processes are highly dependent on government's role in ensuring a proper legal framework for their operation. A requirement for e-government processes to be introduced and adopted is their formal legal equivalence and standing with the paper process. Additionally, current public governance frameworks based on the assumption that agencies work alone (in terms of performance management, accountability frameworks, data sharing for example) can act to inhibit collaboration and information sharing between organisations. Complexity of regulations and requirements on agencies can be another barrier; if agencies are unable to determine what is required of them, they are likely to be unwilling to invest in a project that may not conform with requirements. Finally, privacy and security need to be ensured before e-government initiatives can advance.

The rules and regulations around ICT use can build up, and impose resource obligations on agencies. Given the pervasive nature of ICT use in government, these requirements can cover acquisition and financing, network operations and security, staffing and skills issues, service design, monitoring and reporting. They are likely to have been issued by a number of agencies, rather than a single agency or the central e-government co-ordinating unit. It would be of value to regularly undertake a review of the overall regulations and requirements that govern ICT acquisition and use. As a first step, identifying these would help indicate areas where redundant or overlapping regulations were in place: an agreed process of regular examination would provide an opportunity to get rid of requirements that have outlived their usefulness.

Recognition of e-government processes

The introduction and uptake of e-government services and processes will remain minimal without a legal equivalence between digital and paper processes. OECD governments are aware of the need for a framework to provide for enforceable electronic transactions, both in the e-government sphere and for electronic commerce, and have taken action.

For example, the legal recognition of digital signatures is necessary if they are to be used in e-government for the submission of electronic forms containing sensitive personal or financial information. As of 2002, 26 of the 30 OECD countries have passed legislation recognising digital signatures, though a much smaller number have actually introduced applications beyond a pilot phase. Many are waiting for the private sector to fill the void.

In response to a Ministerial mandate, the OECD Working Party on Information Security and Privacy (WPISP) is preparing a survey to assess cross-jurisdictional challenges and impediments associated with authentication services. From this survey, information will be compiled on domestic legislative/legal/policy frameworks for electronic authentication and findings gathered on regulations applicable to entities providing authentication services. On this basis, the exercise will help determine how varying legislative/legal/policy frameworks can be bridged to provide for cross-jurisdictional acceptance of authentication services and provide for legal effect of electronic signatures.

Complexity of requirements

Confusion about what exactly are the requirements on agencies implementing e-government is another problem. Agencies may need clarification on what they should and should not do, particularly in the areas of data security and technical standards. Especially in the case of small agencies with few resources, the cost of re-developing an e-government project which has adopted the wrong standards is potentially prohibitive. A vicious circle may occur when ignorance of current regulations leads to incorrect development of e-government projects and to waste of resources, and in turn results in more regulation.

The web of government requirements around ICT procurement, industry support, contract requirements, compliance with security requirements and

Box 13.   **Digital Signatures in OECD Countries**

	Status of e-signature legislation
Australia	Enacted
Austria	Enacted
Belgium	Enacted
Canada	Enacted
Czech Republic	Enacted
Denmark	Enacted
Finland	Draft bill
France	Enacted
Germany	Enacted
Greece	Enacted
Hungary	Enacted
Iceland	Enacted
Ireland	Enacted
Italy	Enacted
Japan	Enacted
Korea	Enacted
Luxembourg	Enacted
Mexico	Proposed draft
Netherlands	Pending
New Zealand	Enacted
Norway	Enacted
Poland	Enacted
Portugal	Enacted
Slovak Republic	Enacted
Spain	Enacted
Sweeden	Enacted
Switzerland	Experimental regulation[1]
Turkey	Draft bill
United Kingdom	Enacted
United States	Enacted

1. Though Switzerland has made major efforts to catch up with the development of e-government related legislation, the process towards the recognition of a full legislation on e-signature is still ongoing. A law recognizing the equivalence between traditional and electronic signature has not yet been enacted. An experimental regulation (decree) has been issued regarding the conditions under which certification service providers may be recognized on a voluntary basis. The scope of the decree is to promote the provision of secure electronic certification services to a wide public and encourage the use and the legal recognition of digital signatures.

Source: OECD based on data from *www.bmck.com/home-transactions.htm*

other standards can increase costs and drag out implementation timetables. Seamless government services involving a number of agencies unavoidably add to the complexity of implementation.

Combining existing requirements with clear informal/regulatory guidance is a primary challenge to e-government co-ordinators. Government should address how existing regulations should be clarified and explained to e-governments implementers' and in turn impact the implementation of services.

Collaboration frameworks

E-government has the potential to improve collaboration across agencies and organisations, but there are a number of regulatory barriers to collaboration. For example accountability rules, designed to ensure responsible use of public resources by clearly identifying who does what, can impede collaboration as it may be unclear who is accountable for shared projects. Similarly, performance management follows clear distinctions of who did what, and there is little flexibility for evaluating shared projects. Finally, legislation enacted in order to protect the privacy and security of citizens' data can impede data sharing across government (see below).

Privacy and security

Citizens are unlikely to use e-government services without a guarantee of privacy and security. Governments also have a strong interest in maintaining citizens' trust (*e.g.* that information provided will not be misused). The difficulty of protecting individual privacy can be an important barrier to e-government implementation. Ensuring that e-government initiatives are in step with society's expectations in this area is a crucial means of building trust. The challenge facing e-government coordinators and implementers is to respect accepted privacy principles while allowing the benefits of the Internet and other technologies to flow to citizens. This balance is of particular importance when considering seamless government services involving data sharing among agencies.

Government has a responsibility to provide leadership in developing a culture of privacy protection and security. IT should provide this leadership through its roles in the development of public policy, as owner and operator of systems and networks, and as a user of such systems and networks. As a user of information systems and networks, government shares a role with businesses, other organisations and individuals for ensuring secure use of the system and network.

The OECD was the first intergovernmental organisation to issue guidelines on international policy for the protection of privacy in computerised data processing. In 1980, the Guidelines on the Protection of Privacy and Transborder Flows of Personal Data (Privacy Guidelines) were adopted as a Recommendation of the OECD Council. They were followed by

Box 14.   France: Protection of privacy with regard to the need for links between electronic files

France's chief priority has been to protect privacy in response to the threat posed by the expansion of electronic files and the potential uses of new information and communications technologies (NICT), and in particular the possibility of matching files which contain personal data. At the same time, some countries have sought to use NICT to simplify administrative formalities by connecting various files so as to minimise the need to ask citizens to supply the same personal data several times. Other countries have sought to make their administration more efficient by authorising it to match information on the same individual. France is not opposed to endeavouring to deliver administrative services more efficiently to the citizen, nor to simplifying administrative formalities; it requires only that constant care be taken to ensure that the rights of the individual are safeguarded when automatic processing of personal data is introduced.

The Law of 6 January 1978 "*Informatique et libertés*" recognises that individuals have a number of rights in regard to the automatic processing of personal data by the public and private sectors, as does most of the legislation on data protection, and the Council of Europe Convention No.108 for the protection of individuals with regard to automatic processing of personal data, which was ratified by France. These rights are: the right of individuals to ask anybody whether it holds information concerning them, to have knowledge of that information, either directly or indirectly through an intermediary in the case of data concerning national defence or public safety for example, the right to rectify data, to refuse that a file be kept on them when such a file is not obligatory by law, or the "right to be forgotten", which allows individuals to request that certain non-permanent personal data concerning them be removed from a file.

Another fundamental right is that bodies wishing to introduce the automatic processing of personal data must inform individuals in advance of the use that will be made of the data concerning them. Prior to implementing any computerised data processing project, an administration must submit it for an opinion (or declare it, in the case of the most routine processing) to the *Commission Nationale de l'Informatique et des Libertés* (CNIL *www.cnil.fr.index.htm*), a body set up by the Law of 6 January 1978. The CNIL examines the proposed uses of the data and ensures that there is transparency, so that the individuals concerned can exercise their various rights.

The administration responsible for processing personal information must inform the CNIL of the aim(s) of the processing it wishes to introduce, in order to obtain its opinion. It must also specify the data that will be recorded for the purpose of that aim, how long they will be stored and the categories of persons who will have access to them. The content of the processing must correspond to the declared aim and must not be used for other purposes, under pain of constituting a criminally punishable offence. This means that the purpose of a file that would be shared several administrations must be clearly specified and receive a favourable opinion from the CNIL.

THE E-GOVERNMENT IMPERATIVE – ISBN 92-64-10117-9 – © OECD 2003

> **Box 14. France: Protection of privacy with regard to the need for links between electronic files** (*cont.*)
>
> One of the government's priorities is to facilitate citizens' access to the administration by reducing the number of agencies they have to deal with, by simplifying administrative formalities, by reducing the time it takes to deals with requests, and by making the administration more user-friendly. In accordance with the measures of the Law "*Informatique et libertés*" of 6 January 1978, a personalised citizen's portal is being launched "*mon.service-public.fr.*" This portal will eventually allow the user to obtain a personal set of information and online services, either anonymously or personalised as the case may be. The objective is to support the development of e-government by progressively building personalised portals and electronic user accounts so as to allow citizens to access records containing their personal information and to facilitate citizens contacts and relations with the administration.
>
> *Source*: OECD E-Government Working Group.

the 1985 Declaration on Transborder Data Flows, and more recently by the Ministerial Declaration on the Protection of Privacy on Global Networks, adopted by OECD Ministers at the 1998 Ottawa conference, "A Borderless World: Realising the Potential of Global Electronic Commerce". At that conference, OECD Ministers reaffirmed "their commitment to the protection of privacy on global networks in order to ensure the respect of important rights, build confidence in global networks, and to prevent unnecessary restrictions on transborder flows of personal data".

The revised *OECD Guidelines for the Security of Information Systems and Networks: Towards a Culture of Security* that were adopted by the OECD Council in July 2002, respond to the ever-changing nature of the security environment by promoting the development of a culture of security – that is, a focus on security in the development of information systems and networks and the adoption of new ways of thinking and behaving by all participants when using information systems and communicating or transacting across networks.

3.2. Budgetary barriers

OECD governments operate within vertical funding structures, in accordance with the core public management principle of holding an agency accountable for achieving organisational objectives and giving it the resources to accomplish those objectives. However, such budgetary frameworks may not take into account the specific needs of certain e-government projects, particularly those involving long-term funding requirements and collaboration across agencies. In order to maximise the benefits of e-government financing issues must be addressed.

One commentator (Harvard Policy Group) considers there is a virtually inverse relationship between traditional government budgeting and ICT investments.

Table 1. **Traditional budgeting and budgeting for ICT investments**

Focus of traditional government budgeting	Characteristics of high-value ICT investments
Single-year (or biennial) expenditures	Multi-year investments
Programme-by-programme performance	Enterprise or cross-boundary performance
Financial cost/benefits	Financial and non-financial costs/benefits
Level of effort within existing work flows	Changes in the flow of work
Ongoing operations	"Start-up" operations
Control	Innovation

Source: Harvard Policy Group (2001).

Specific budgetary issues

A number of features of current budgetary arrangements in OECD countries work against efficient implementation of e-government. Current budgetary frameworks provide financing for individual projects, but do little to account for the shared responsibility inherent in many e-government projects.

E-government funding:

- To the extent that an explicit choice is made, the implementation of e-government is often unlikely to win out in competition with other compelling public policy objectives such as education, security and health. While most e-government proposals will be argued for in terms of programme outcomes rather than in terms of advancing e-government *per se*, the **level of resources** devoted to e-government is ultimately a matter for governments to determine in the light of their overall priorities.

- The difficulty of measuring costs and potential benefits for e-government projects makes it hard to develop funding cases for projects and compare alternatives in a budget-setting context.

- The treatment of certain ICT spending as capital rather than recurrent expenditure is a major challenge. Not all ICT expenditure is of a capital or investment nature, but involves maintenance, associated recurrent staffing costs, or small-scale projects. However, if major projects are not considered as investment, they will need to compete with other more pressing recurrent funding proposals, and in this context will seem to involve large levels of expenditure.

● Budget time horizons can pose problems for e-government. Many e-government projects will be multi-year in nature, and thus require commitments to spend resources over a long period, sometimes well beyond the annual or multi-year budgeting horizon. Such projects represent a commitment to spend future revenues, and governments are understandably reluctant to tie up future spending. Projects that do not require such a commitment may be favoured.

E-government collaboration:

● There are a number of **budgetary rigidities** that prevent shared funding arrangements. The vertical nature of current arrangements means that it can be difficult to request joint funding, to pay into a project being done by another agency, or to pool funds. There are few mechanisms for shared funding, and it can be difficult to assess the extent to which agencies are benefiting from (and hence should contribute to) a shared project.

● The use of **performance-based budgeting** can create disincentives for collaboration, by rewarding independent behaviour at the expense of shared projects (see section on legislative and regulatory barriers).

● There is no framework for **profit sharing**. Agencies have no incentives to eliminate redundant systems by sharing systems with other agencies unless they can share in some of the savings generated.

Possible solutions

A number of steps can be taken to help overcome the aforementioned budgetary barriers. **E-government funding** can be assisted by the following measures:

● Major ICT projects could be usefully **classified as capital investment**, involving a single or a series of up-front capital outlays, with a consequent stream of benefits. This would enable a fairer comparison of such proposals with recurrent spending alternatives, or in some systems remove the capital project from recurrent budget frameworks. Classifying such major projects as capital investment help with funding of e-government projects. This will also help with problems of budget time horizons.

● In a number of countries, spending on e-government requires **separate** approval by the e-government co-ordinating office to ensure that there is no duplication or inconsistency with broader strategies and architectures. Clear rules and structured consultation processes will help maintain agency confidence in this approach.

- **Public-private partnerships** can be used to bypass budgetary constraints and thus respond to a number of barriers, including obtaining capital, budget-time horizons and disincentives for innovation and collaboration. For example, using a private partner to build the required infrastructure, and then leasing it, or otherwise paying on a user-pays basis will reduce the need for up-front capital, but with the risk of greater long-term cost.

- Specific central **funding for innovation** can be used to fund innovative and high-risk demonstrations that otherwise would not receive funding. Arrangements could be used to augment this funding though linked (or matching funds) from other agencies, private partners, or by using seed financing from a central fund with the expectation that the investment will be repaid (in part or in full).

- An agreed approach to the **assessment of costs and benefits** of e-government can help evaluate and fund successful projects (see section on Monitoring and Evaluation).

- The ability of agencies to **retain savings** generated from e-government initiatives will be important as an incentive for agencies to look for efficiencies.

The linked nature of many e-government projects across traditional programme and organisational lines means that shared budgetary arrangements are essential. On the basis that the bulk of funds for e-government will (and should) be provided through agency budgets, the budget process can be used to promote co-ordination of e-government initiatives. **E-government collaboration** can be aided by the following measures:

- A **central register** of e-government initiatives seeking funding would enable agencies and e-government co-ordinators to see the range of new proposals and identify potential duplication.

- **Central funds** can be used to encourage certain activities, such as collaborative initiatives by agencies.

- Under the **lead agency model**, an agency funds a project that benefits other agencies as well as itself.

- Another possibility is that a number of **agencies co-ordinate their approach** to obtaining funds. This may be done, for example, by dividing a project into segments. (However, this approach can lead to implementation problems regarding the division of the project, especially as some agencies may be successful in obtaining funding while others fail.)

- Under **pooled funding** arrangements, agencies share funding for a common project. It is important to be able to formalise such arrangements in quasi-contractual arrangements, to provide clarity for all parties and to allow for a unified project management and implementation approach.

Box 15. **United Kingdom: Innovative funding mechanisms**

In 1998, the government set up a Capital Modernisation Fund, separate from allocations to individual departments, to finance innovative investments based on project proposals. These funds, which were available as a result of under-spending of conventional capital allocations, have been used extensively for ICT projects. According to the Treasury Website, "the Capital Modernisation Fund was set up to support capital investment to improve public services. For 2000-01, GBP 200 million were added to the Fund as part of the Budget 2000 announcement to take the Fund to GBP 2.7 billion between 1999 and 2001-02". Funding is allocated on a competitive basis and on the following criteria:

- Extent to which the project applies genuinely innovative approaches to service delivery.

- Quality and strength of the economic appraisal of the project.

- Impact on the efficiency and effectiveness of the service.

- How far the project contributes to the department's objectives.

- How far the project is genuinely additional.

- Robustness of arrangements for delivering, managing, accounting, monitoring and evaluating the project.

Successful projects have included e-government initiatives. In the first round (1999-2000), e-government projects funded included: GBP 470 million as part of the National IT Strategy to provide 1 000 IT learning centres across the country; GBP 1.1 million in to leverage various e-commerce procurement initiatives, in particular to develop a government "shopping mall" to provide electronic tendering for low-value transactions to and from government which could save over GBP 10 million a year; and GBP 600 000 for electronic procurement by foreign and Commonwealth Office posts overseas. In the second round, GBP 23.3 million were allocated to transform the Crown Court and reduce delay in the criminal justice system by more effective management of cases through the Crown Court while improving the quality of service to court users. This involved: a PC-based system for electronic presentation of evidence, producing significant savings in court time in complex cases; electronic transcripts of court proceedings through a digital audio recording of the official record; and improved distribution of information by displaying relevant information on how cases are progressing on public information kiosks and a read-only access IT source.

Source: OECD E-Government Working Group.

- **Agency payment models** involve arrangements in which the co-ordinating agency funds the development of the project, and agencies that use the service then pay to use it. The advantage of operating on a voluntary basis

Box 16. **Canada: Central funding criteria**

The objective of the Canadian Government Online (GOL) initiative is to encourage the re-engineering and integration of services so as to better meet the needs of individuals and businesses, and to achieve operational and delivery efficiencies within government. Government Online is client-focused and takes a "whole-of-government" view for clients, with significant economies of scale, while still maintaining ministerial accountabilities and responsibilities.

Central funding has been the catalyst for horizontal co-operation among federal departments and extends into other jurisdictions. The ability to transfer incremental funding into departmental accounts has permitted the government to look for collaborative opportunities, sometimes more complicated and expensive up front, but which clearly promise an eventual return on investment stemming from the savings achieved by offering some common solutions, systems and infrastructure to link departments that need them. It has also allowed the government to insist on high standards of documentation, governance and reporting. The centralised approach has accelerated, the successful delivery of Internet-based services, including in departments where tight discretionary budgets did not allow for the early introduction of such capabilities. There is now a large and growing network of key personnel who co-operate outside of departmental boundaries and stimulate the efficient sharing of best practices, technical tools and key lessons learned.

Early projects were carefully screened by interdepartmental review committees and successful projects received appropriate central funding. In most cases, this central funding covered only part of the project's total cost, with the balance contributed by sponsoring departments and their contributing partners. Three examples of successful projects that have substantially benefited from the centralised approach to GOL are:

- Seniors Canada Online, a project led by Veterans Affairs Canada (VAC) and involving multiple partners and jurisdictions, responds to the need for more and better information specifically tailored to the needs and the realistic computer capabilities of Canadian seniors, their families, caregivers, service providers and supporting organisations.

- e-Client Application Status, a project led by Citizenship and Immigration Canada (CIC), allows individuals to check electronically on the status of their immigration applications. This project involves the safeguarding and transmission of personal information and was therefore a logical choice to act as a prototype for a highly secure electronic communications network.

- The Canada Site, a project led by Communications Canada which includes input from virtually all federal departments, is a layered portal comprising three "gateways" and a single point of entry to all information holdings that are pertinent to interactions between government and its various clients. This major undertaking has absorbed large amounts of funding for development, maintenance and marketing, amounts that only became possible with central direction, co-ordination and funding.

Box 16. **Canada: Central funding criteria** (*cont.*)

GOL supports a "whole-of-government" approach by funding departments to work with partners on common solutions. Incremental funding, even if on the margin, can influence the pace or approach to the re-engineering of services by departments. The approach has accelerated the move towards greater horizontal management across departments and opened a new channel for communication and collaboration.

Source: OECD E-Government Working Group.

Box 17. **Italy: The co-ordination of financial resources for e-government**

In 2002 the Italian Ministry for Innovation and Technology launched an initiative for the implementation of e-government at local level to co-finance, (up to € 120 million), projects proposed by the different local governments (regions, provinces, municipalities). A specific objective of the initiative was to co-ordinate the different financial sources so as to maximize the use of the limited financial resources available at central level. To this end, in the call for tender which was launched to select the local government projects to be co-financed, specific criteria were proposed to favour those projects which were coherent with the regional strategic plan for the development of e-government.

In response to these criteria, the proponents of the projects began to co-ordinate their initiatives with the strategic regional plans, while most regional governments provided additional financial resources for the selected projects. Through this mechanism, most of the projects selected were financed from three different financial sources: national funds, regional funds and local administrations funds

Each of these sources represents a specific commitment for the success of the projects. Furthermore, the regions in the South of Italy decided to use the European Union Regional Development structural funds, adding a further strong element of commitment.

To sum up: the use of a call for tender, as opposed to the traditional transfer of funds, brought about a stronger commitment by the local governments who were proposing e-government projects; the requirement for projects to be coherent with regional strategic plans (in addition to being coherent with the national e-government action plan) brought about a convergence of the different financial resources for e-government development.

Source: OECD E-Government Working Group.

is that agencies will join if they feel the service is of value. This approach also incites the co-ordinating agency to meet agency needs.

- **A mandatory levy** on agencies may enable some projects to proceed that otherwise would not. However such a levy could be difficult to negotiate.

- Performance-based budgeting should **take into account shared responsibility** in order to create incentives or shared projects.

Box 18. **United States: "Pass the hat" – pooled agency funding of projects**

The Clinger-Cohen Act (formerly known as the Information Technology Management Reform Act) implicitly encouraged multi-agency projects by directing the Office of Management and Budget (OMB) to issue "guidance for undertaking … multi-agency and government-wide investments in information technology…", thereby prompting the OMB to issue guidance on capital planning as part of its omnibus policy document on information resources, "Managing Information Resources" (OMB Circular No. A-130). The Act also gives OMB the authority to redirect funds from one agency to another to finance multi-agency projects. Finally, the Act permits joint agency funding of projects, known as "pass the hat" funding, a practice otherwise prohibited under most US appropriations laws, which tend to require single agency funding and accountability for projects.

The authority to redirect funds has, until recently, not been used. In May 2002, OMB did invoke this authority in support of an e-government initiative, online rulemaking management. In July 2002, OMB announced its intent to use its Clinger-Cohen authority to support the realignment of government functions envisioned by the Administration's proposed Department of Homeland Security by limiting individual agency investments in projects that will need to be consolidated.

The "pass the hat" authority has also played a role in financing e-government initiatives in at least two important ways. It is being used to finance the activities of the federal Chief Information Officers (CIO) Council (*www.cio.gov*), the principal co-ordinating body for federal ICT activities, and to fund the FirstGov initiative.

Source: OECD E-Government Working Group.

Box 19. **Mexico: Co-ordination of the government budget process**

The Mexican government established SAETI, a system for planning, budgeting and evaluating ICT projects from all federal agencies. The system helps match ICT projects against overarching objectives, detects overlaps and aids in evaluating the performance of ICT investments.

Source: OECD E-Government Working Group.

3.3. Technological change

A number of technological difficulties can impede the implementation of e-government programmes and initiatives. This is a very complex issue, and this section will identify only a fey key issues and very broad solutions. Key issues include legacy systems, shared infrastructure, and lagging behind the rapid pace of new technological developments.

Legacy systems

Governments continue to make considerable ICT investments and at any point in time will have a wide range of ICT systems in place. However, legacy systems (systems that were designed for specific purposes) can be inflexible, and incompatible systems make it hard to deploy new applications that involve the need for data sharing or other interaction between disparate systems. Legacy systems can also lead to increased costs, for example related to data transfer. In fact, the difficulty of integrating legacy systems with new initiatives can be a major barrier to e-government. Integrating back office information management and information processing systems with the Internet to provide an online interface to clients has been a major preoccupation of e-government efforts.

This issue is a complex one, and solutions advanced will develop and change over time. Currently, the need for integrated transactional seamless government services has helped promote the development of middleware solutions and web services, a software integrating technology incorporating standards such as Extensible Markup Language (XML) which facilitate the exchange of data between different systems. The promotion of whole of government frameworks, standards and data definitions by e-government co-ordinators will facilitate specific proposals to develop cross agency integrated services.

Shared infrastructure

A lack of shared standards and compatible infrastructure between departments and agencies can impede inter-agency collaboration and the uptake of e-government. But the expense of implementing modern infrastructure can be a major barrier to the implementation of e-government initiatives. Shared infrastructure among agencies is one way of overcoming this problem. However, the development of shared infrastructure can be difficult because of budgetary constraints (see section 3.2), and the difficulties of collaboration.

Government can help by providing a technological framework for delivering electronic services. Establishing common technical standards and infrastructure can pave the way for greater efficiency within government. Important economies can be gained through a whole-of-government approach, both in terms of reducing redundant systems and by lowering the legal and technological barriers for co-operation across organisations. A national approach may range from shared systems to common rules and/or standards governing separate, but connected systems. For example, governments can benefit from scale economies for some common back-office processes, such as human resources management and payroll.

Box 20.   **Finland: Shared infrastructure**

Large-scale or cross-agency e-government initiatives in Finland have usually been planned by or at least have had heavy involvement and/or support from either the Ministry of Finance or the Ministry of the Interior. These ministries can act as a catalyst as well as a formal or informal mediator for the interests of the participating agencies. For example, the JUNA project, the citizen ID card, the citizen portal and the TYVI project all originated in either the Ministry of the Interior or the Ministry of Finance.

In Finland, interoperability work is carried out through JUHTA, the Advisory Committee on Information Management in Public Administration. So far, JUHTA has set over 40 IT standards. There is bound to be frustration, however, as there will always be a lag between the changes in the technical system, services and technological possibilities and the rules governing them.

Source: OECD report on E-Government in Finland (2003).

Preparing for technological change

Governments face the challenge of fostering the development of e-government while there is still great uncertainty regarding fast moving technological change, and it is difficult to anticipate future policy impacts in detail. One approach to dealing with technological risk is to partner with the private sector. But such partnerships are difficult when governments are trying to establish standards that may not yet be established in the market (see box on Finland Smart Card Case, below).

Broad approaches to dealing with emerging technologies include (OECD 2002a):

- Technology neutrality in legislation and regulation to avoid closing off promising options.
- Flexibility within broad regulatory frameworks and adaptation of current laws to a digital world.
- Involvement of all stakeholders in regulatory processes.
- Performance requirements rather than technical specifications when procuring new technologies.
- Increasingly looking to international co-operation to harmonise approaches to transborder issues.

Box 21. **Finland: Smart card case**

The Finnish electronic identity card is a smart card that replaces the existing citizen identification card with a smartcard that serves all of the identity card's previous functions while adding new electronic capacities: it can be used for electronic identification and digital signatures, as a tool for encrypting sensitive documents and as an enabler for information exchange among citizens, business and public authorities, as well as for secure electronic transactions.

One reason for the relatively weak uptake of the card is the lack of public-private collaboration in developing user solutions and interactive services for the card. Higher public security standards (stronger data encryption) did not take into consideration either the development of private market technologies or the desired and actual needs of the potential users. The result has been the fairly limited development of electronic service and the under-utilisation of the card.

Co-operation with the private sectors in developing electronic applications for the card may have helped broaden not only the user base, but may have also brought the additional benefits of breaking up technological barriers and establishing a common framework for developing applications.

Source: OECD report on E-Government in Finland (2003).

3.4. The digital divide

The digital divide is a barrier to e-government in that people who do not have access to the Internet will be unable to benefit from online services (OECD 2002a). In OECD countries a growing number of people have access to the Internet, but there are still large numbers of people who do not (see Figure 1 and Annex 3). While e-government can also improve services to citizens through other channels (notably by improving back office procedures), the inability to provide online services to all citizens can hold back e-government projects.

Figure 1. **Households with access to Internet, 2000 and 2001**

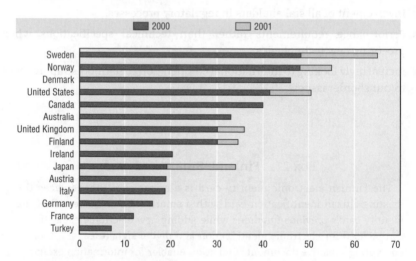

Note: For Denmark, Ireland and the United Kingdom, access to the Internet via a home computer; for the other countries access to the Internet through any device (e.g. computer, phone, TV, etc.). 2001 for selected countries only.
Source: OECD IT Outlook 2002, based on ICT database and national sources.

Additionally, the groups in society with lower levels of access tend to be those that are already disadvantaged. For example, lower income groups have less access to the Internet than higher income groups. Such disadvantaged groups are often the targets of government interventions and have a higher level of ongoing interaction with government. Many of their interactions with government are complex – establishing identity, entitlement for assistance, complex medical or social intervention – and they are not all well suited to online provision. While access to government information and services would be important for such groups, they may not benefit from enhancements to service quality and greater choice through online services.

THE E-GOVERNMENT IMPERATIVE – ISBN 92-64-10117-9 – © OECD 2003

E-government services may by their very existence encourage individuals to access the Internet. However, for most citizens, transactions with government are relatively rare and will not generally provide households with the main incentive to purchase a PC and Internet connection. However, government information and opportunities for consultation and participation, particularly at the local level, may be important in conjunction with other factors such as educational uses, access to e-mail and messaging and home PC use. It is thus important, on e-government grounds alone, for governments to continue policies and specific interventions to reduce the digital divide. A specific focus on frequently used government services with value to groups with low access, along with overall marketing of online government services, could be an important element of digital divide policies.

ISBN 92-64-10117-9
The E-Government Imperative
© OECD 2003

Chapter 4

Implementing E-Government

Capturing the potential benefits of e-government is challenging OECD member countries to take a more co-ordinated approach to its implementation. Governments are actively engaged in developing policies and plans and rolling out e-government initiatives, as well as co-ordinating existing initiatives in order to improve the integration of services. The incorporation of the Internet into the mix of technologies has clearly provided an impetus to ICT use in government and provided new solutions, but has also raised new problems.

Most member countries have established or are establishing new organisational units to facilitate e-government implementation. Others have added these responsibilities to established structures. While actual responsibilities may differ, the relevant units face a central challenge of finding a balance between, on the one hand, meeting the need for improving co-ordination and shared approaches and, on the other hand, continuing to foster flexibility, innovation and individual responsibility.

Given the complexity and breadth of implementation issues, the OECD E-Government Working Group focused on issues faced by all members for implementing e-government. E-government places a high priority on improving services and increasing citizen engagement in the policy making process. But the related and essential reform of the administrative back-office (including issues such as organisational change, leadership, central co-ordination, collaboration and seamless government services, e-government skills, public-private partnerships, managing risk and cost and monitoring and evaluation) demands a whole-of-government approach and will be one of the most challenging areas for e-government.

4.1. Vision statement and plan

A vision statement and plan can help administrations set a course at the start, monitor progress forthrightly, help orient individual initiatives and make numerous mid-course corrections. Where possible, e-government should encompass a vision statement, broad objectives at national level, and a planning process with specific goals and targets.

Vision statements

A common vision is essential to e-government as a means to engage and co-ordinate agencies. A shared vision also serves to engage political leaders and to impress upon them the importance of e-government. A common vision is not a goal in itself, but a means to achieve policy priorities.

In OECD countries, most advanced e-government organisations have a vision statement. Such a statement may be linked to political commitment at a higher level, or it may be dependent on a general manager or the head of an IT unit with sufficient determination and resources. Whether the vision is shared across the government or is limited to an individual organisation, however, makes a significant difference. No matter how advanced they are in terms of the services that they provide, organisations dependent on their own vision may not be aware of co-ordination problems that extend beyond their own services.

A government-wide vision helps to tie e-government initiatives with broader strategic and reform objectives. A vision statement can help promote inter-ministerial co-ordination, ensure balance and fairness and help to stay the course over a number of years. Having a clear vision of reform helps to maintain consistency and a sense of purpose. Towards this end, political leaders are key supporters of an e-government vision. Political leadership serves to diffuse the vision and to give it added weight. While a vision statement is needed, it is not enough, and the vision, the rationale and the validation for reform need to be communicated to the administration.

The most effective e-government visions depend on input from a variety of stakeholders. Increasingly, users (both citizens and business), non-governmental organisations, and government employees are being brought into the process of defining an e-government vision. This serves to ensure ownership of an e-government vision and to make sure that it can be translated into realistic action plans.

Box 22. **Mexico: Good government agenda**

President Vicente Fox of Mexico established a good government agenda with six major lines of action, one of them being e-government and all of them related to each other. Each year, the president negotiates with the head of every agency the performance targets for the agenda, which includes e-government objectives and targets, as well as the effect of the latter on savings, quality, innovation and transparency. After several decades of mistrust by the public and general corruption, the government of Mexico faces the big challenge of changing its culture rapidly and effectively. In 2001 it produced its code of ethics that has been taught online to practically all federal government middle and senior level managers.

Source: OECD E-Government Working Group.

E-government objectives

E-government objectives are distinguishable from the more general vision in that they translate the broad values contained in the vision into more concrete outcomes, usually with a stronger operational basis, reflecting actual programmes, procedures or outputs. They can either indicate a broad goal or desired programme direction (*e.g.* serve more citizens) or a more specific target (*e.g.* "serve all eligible citizens by 2005"). Objectives can therefore form a planning hierarchy in which organisations set specific targets in support of broader government goals that help to achieve the overall e-government vision.

The e-government planning process within the central government helps to establish and diffuse the vision and to translate it into goals and targets. Goals serve not only to provide a direction for action and achievement, they can also be used to prioritise and even advance action. Government-wide planning and the setting of objectives can also improve co-ordination between government organisations, serve to establish criteria for reconciling conflicting approaches and signal preferred approaches and shared resources for overcoming challenges.

Objectives can be set at the national, ministry, agency or project level, taking into account the specificity of each sector or organisation. For example, some countries have chosen quite specific goals at the national level in order to create pressure to advance their e-government initiatives. Objectives at the national level can be used to:

- Secure support, involvement and responsibility from the top political and management level in all ministries.
- Ensure the necessary legislation and central funding.
- Create useful co-ordination and co-operation mechanisms.
- Ensure motivation/incentives for cross-administration projects.
- Ensure that targets are integrated into performance and budget management processes to create/facilitate ministerial steering mechanisms.
- Ensure ownership/responsibility at the central level for overall co-ordination, monitoring and evaluation of national strategy.
- Ensure that the steering of the national vertical strategy is integrated with the horizontal steering of administrative fields (to address the decentralisation/centralisation dilemma).

Without milestones to measure the achievement of goals, there is less overall pressure for agencies to act. Without clear targets, ministries and agencies may have difficulty knowing what they need to do or how to

> ### Box 23. Germany: The E-Government Manual as the way to effective and efficient e-government
>
> The major focus of the German initiative "BundOnline 2005" (*www.bund.de/bundonline2005*) is an ambitious plan to develop a standardised and far-reaching e-government infrastructure in Germany. In order to achieve this demanding goal within a limited amount of time, Germany has preferred to rely on existing resources when developing and implementing e-government processes. More and more public administrations are moving towards electronic processes based on information and communication technology (ICT). In view of the specific requirements these processes must fulfil, especially concerning accuracy, IT security is increasingly important. Therefore, IT security requirements deserve special attention when public administration business processes are being (re)designed. Using ICT has the potential to optimise processes – but much depends on whether the existing processes and underlying structures are organised and optimised to meet needs such as effectiveness and usability. Hence, the driving force behind these activities is the people responsible for process redesign.
>
> In addition to expert legal knowledge and skills in ICT disciplines, a crucial factor for success is managing e-government as a project within each government agency. As part of the German master plan for e-government, the E-Government Manual is an instrument to help train, qualify and increase the awareness of e-government teams. The manual focuses on best practices and pragmatic approaches to integrating security aspects at the beginning of an e-government project. One important target is to motivate all those involved in these activities to ensure a solid foundation for secure e-government.
>
> The E-Government Manual consists of a set of modules written for different clienteles such as senior management, e-government officers and ICT security experts. It offers guidance on how to develop and implement e-government processes and describes several technical and non-technical solutions. Each of the various authors is an expert in his field.
>
> *Related Source*: "E-Government Handbuch", Bonn; *Bundesamt für Sicherheit in der Informationstechnik/* Federal Office for Information Security, *www.e-government-manual.de*

prioritise their actions. If goals are the bridge between an overall vision and specific action, what is sometimes perceived as a lack of e-government vision and strategy may actually reflect a lack of clear goals and targets.

Many countries have issued targets as a central element of their e-government strategies, with common targets for placing services online by a specified date. These can be important as a way of generating momentum

> ## Box 24. **European Commission: eEurope objectives**
>
> The European Commission has played an important role in identifying the actual and potential benefits of the information society and acting as a stimulus to ensure that all members continue to advance in this area. The eEurope programme is a political initiative aimed at "bringing every citizen, home and school, every business and administration, into the digital age and online; creating a digitally literate Europe, supported by an entrepreneurial culture ready to finance and develop new ideas; ensuring the whole process is socially inclusive, builds consumer trust and strengthens social cohesion".
>
> In order to achieve these goals, the eEurope programme has defined priority actions and set targets for providing IT training to young people, providing cheap and fast access to the Internet, accelerating e-commerce, developing safe authentication systems for citizens (smart cards), enhancing e-participation for the disabled, improving health care online and strengthening e-government. As in other areas, specific targets for e-government have been set (*i.e.* simplify online public information) for electronic information and service provision, and indicators have been developed to measure countries' efforts towards achieving these goals.
>
> *Source*: eEurope, "An Information Society for All", Communication on a Commission Initiative for the Special European Council of Lisbon, 23 and 24 March 2000.

and gaining public engagement. However, missing these targets, or even perceptions that they will be missed can sour public perceptions. Dealing with this can require much energy and attention. A problem can also arise from the necessarily long timeframes for meeting ambitious targets. Targets themselves may become somewhat outdated and cease to reflect newer thinking and policy development; the lock-in involved in such targets may be inconsistent with Internet time cycles of change.

In reality, many national targets are based on inadequate information about citizen demand, government resources and technological developments. Without a plan on how to achieve them, broad targets are not particularly useful and may even be counter-productive if too unrealistic. They should be distinguished, however, from more specific, short-term targets that build on each other and are negotiated with ministries and agencies or developed in consultation. Such targets can be useful tools to advance action, secure leadership buy-in and improve accountability.

Performance measures, within the framework of national vision and goals, can also serve to improve accountability by offering indicators against which to measure performance (see section on monitoring and evaluation).

> ### Box 25.   **Finland: Explicit goals**
>
> Almost all agencies and ministries in Finland responding to the OECD survey used for the report "E-Government in Finland" reported including explicit goals in their e-government plans (90%), and most also include an explicit strategy on how to reach those goals (87%). Evaluation plans and frameworks for monitoring goals were less common. Over half of respondents reported that their plans stated how to monitor goals. Even fewer (50%) included an evaluation framework.
>
> *Source*: OECD report on E-Government in Finland (2003).

4.2. Front office

The term "front office" refers to government as its constituents see it, meaning the information and services provided and the interaction between government and both citizens and business. Implementation of e-government initiatives concerns two areas regarding the front office: implementation of online services and engagement of citizens.

Online services

In order to survey online services, for the purposes of OECD country reviews such as the review "E-Government in Finland", the OECD adapted a model for electronic service delivery from the Australian National Audit Office.[1] Several international surveys about e-service development have been carried out using a similar model, but there is no general agreement on how to define the stages of online service delivery. In particular, the definition of the last, and supposedly most advanced, stage, seems to cause the most difficulty. This is not surprising given the limited experience with online services at this stage.[2] The Australian model defines four possible stages of online service delivery:

Stage 1: Information. A Website that publishes information about service(s). Since this stage primarily involves the digitising of available information and making it available online, it has required, to date, the least investment in process re-engineering.

Stage 2: Interactive information. Stage 1 plus users' ability to access organisations' database(s) and to browse, explore and interact with that data. While stage 1 information tends to be static, developing services to stage 2 allows users to access an organisation's database for publicly available information and to interact with the information to do electronic searches and

Figure 2. **Stages of online service delivery and core service delivery objectives**

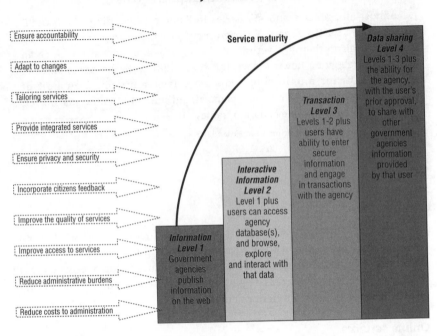

Source: OECD.

calculations based on their own criteria. Both stage 1 and stage 2 services focus on providing information to users. However, stage 2 services necessitate a greater investment in thinking about how citizens and information will use that information, about the rules for making certain information public and accessible, and about the target audience and the types of tools that can add value to the user experience, making it easier to find what he or she is looking for and/or tailoring information searches.

Stage 3: Transactions. Stages 1 and 2 plus users' ability to enter secure information and engage in transactions with the organisation. Developing online services to stage 3 makes it possible for customers to enter secure information and engage in electronic transactions. This stage of service delivery requires real-time responsiveness by government agencies to the service demands of citizens and businesses. It requires therefore that agencies rethink online services standards, security and privacy protection, back-office processes and relations among agencies for seamless service delivery.

Stage 4: Data sharing. Stages 1, 2 and 3 plus the organisation's ability to share with other government organisations personal information, when

THE E-GOVERNMENT IMPERATIVE – ISBN 92-64-10117-9 – © OECD 2003

approved by law and/or with the user's prior consent. It is particularly difficult to define a model for e-service delivery with regard to such advanced online services. In certain countries, sharing data among ministries or agencies is limited because of privacy protection legislation (see section on barriers). Yet data sharing can create significant savings in public administrations and help ease procedures and the reporting burden for citizens and business. All data matching needs to be legally approved or explicitly permitted so as to prevent the unauthorised or illegal combination of data (including anonymous data collection for research). The level of transparency of data-collecting organisations and confidence in data protection authorities are critical both for the accuracy and quality of data and for the protection of citizens' rights.

Service quality

Ensuring service quality is important, both online and offline. Successful services are built on an understanding of user requirements. The initial rollout of online services has experienced some difficulties, but there is now an increasing amount of data on what works and what does not.

Effective services need not be complex. Information services can provide high levels of user value, with only a small additional value flowing from the ability to complete related transactions online. The various stages of online service may imply that it is obligatory to proceed to complex transactions as rapidly as possible and that a country's e-government rating will suffer if this does not occur. However, an understanding of user demand and preferences is necessary. Sometimes simple and correct information meets the needs of users, and moving to the transactional service stage will not necessarily add great value.

The adequacy for online services of existing administrative appeal and scrutiny mechanisms may need to be addressed. The argument that online services need to be integrated into broader frameworks support the view that existing arrangements for scrutiny should cover online service provision. A review of the adequacy of existing arrangements and, in particular, the competencies required for effective oversight may be useful.

Seamless services are likely to be more effective than delivering separate services to the same customer group. While online services provide greater opportunities for integration than other delivery mechanisms, the development of joined-up services within a broader service channel strategy can provide the opportunity for both effective and efficient service delivery (see below).

Box 26. **Denmark: User feedback mechanisms**

The project "Top of the Web" carries out an annual evaluation of all public sector Websites and users' opinions on the services. Public assessments of Websites inspire government institutions to improve the quality of service they provide to citizens. Few public institutions want to rank at the bottom of the list. The Top of the Web evaluation uses a series of criteria to define the characteristics of a high-quality government Website. The evaluation is based on user friendliness, practical value and openness.

User-friendliness: Users should find their way around the site effortlessly regardless of their level of expertise.

Practical value: Users should benefit from the information given, which must be up to date and offer users relevant self-service options.

Openness: Users should understand who takes decisions and how they can influence a decision-making process. Promoting openness also involves meeting users' needs, *e.g.* by enabling them to ask questions and receive answers electronically.

Source: OECD E-Government Working Group.

Channel strategy

E-government services clearly need to be developed as part of a broader service channel strategy, especially given the digital divide. Setting goals to place services online has helped broaden the choice of services available to users. However, implementing these services by integrating them with other channels as part of an overall transformation of a particular service makes it possible to take a structured approach to meeting the needs of particular customer groups. This approach is essential for customer-focused services. It also makes it possible to put the use of online services into context, with the online service channel a complementary access point rather than in competition with more established approaches. An integrated approach is also more efficient in the longer term, as more intensive use can be made of common infrastructure and data.

The need to preserve choice is fundamental to any customer-focused strategy. Providing alternative delivery channels (*e.g.* phone, kiosks, counter, etc.) and indeed choice of online access points will improve chances of ensuring access and effectiveness. Choice of approach is in itself valuable to service quality. The principle of "no wrong door" to access government services should be adopted.

Box 27. **Finland: Channel strategy**

Reactions to the Finnish government's experiments with limiting some traditional delivery channels in certain instances are being closely watched. Two examples:

- The hard copy and disk versions of the citizen's handbook, a Finnish information resource, were eliminated once it was made online. The reason was to ensure that information communicated was always up to date. In justifying this decision, the Ministry of Finance reports that it has more than doubled the number of users with online access to the citizen portal compared to those who had access to the citizen's handbook.

- As part of a 1999 agreement in the JUHTA project to expand the electronic collection of data, Statistics Finland now requires compulsory schools to answer a questionnaire by using the Internet and has developed a collection of Web-based forms for the questionnaire. The decision was taken in consultation with schools, taking into account their needs and Web access. The results have been positive and Statistics Finland is also likely to test a single-channel strategy for the collection of financial information from municipalities.

Source: OECD report on E-Government in Finland (2003).

Citizen engagement[3]

ICT can be used as tools for providing information, consulting and engaging citizens in policy making. The objective of technology-enabled information dissemination, consultation and participation is to improve the policy-making process through a range of devices (Macintosh, 2002):

- Reach and engage with a wider audience to enable broader participation.

- Provide relevant information in a format that is more accessible and more understandable to the target audience to enable more informed participation (for example, making online content available to the disabled, see box below).

- Engage with a wider audience through a range of consultation and participation technologies to take into account the diverse technical and communicative skills of citizens.

- Facilitate the analysis of contributions to support policy makers and to improve policy.

- Provide relevant and appropriate feedback to citizens to ensure openness and transparency in the policy-making process.

- Monitor and evaluate the process to ensure continuous improvement.

Box 28. Canada: Government-wide multi-channel service transformation

Initially, Canada's Government Online (GOL) project focused solely on the provision of electronic services via the Internet. However, to respond to individuals' and businesses' preferences and expectations, the initiative has adopted a broader vision focusing on client-centred service delivery across the range of service delivery channels (Internet, in person, telephone). This demands a much higher degree of co-ordination and integration across the whole of government, and Canada is now pursuing an approach that views the electronic channel as the enabler for delivering multi-channel service improvement. This also requires a number of government-wide strategies to ensure client-centred, responsive, cost-effective, accessible, trusted and secure service delivery. Changes have been made in the GOL and service initiatives' governance structure to promote the shift towards a broader multi-channel service vision and pave the way for long-term governance of more integrated service delivery. The interdepartmental committee structure that oversees GOL has been enhanced to include the multi-channel service concept, and the committees that support the senior level governance committees have received a broader mandate.

Work has been carried out over the past year to support multi-channel service improvement and delivery of key online services in five key areas:

- **Service transformation and multi-channel integration:** pursuing a user-centred approach to electronic, in person and telephone service delivery, driven by client priorities and expectations.

- **Common, secure infrastructure:** building the enterprise-wide electronic service platform that enables integrated services and supports secure Internet, telephone and in-person access.

- **Policy and standards frameworks:** addressing privacy and security with respect to information management to build confidence in online services and link transformation of services to client satisfaction.

- **Communications and marketing:** encouraging the take-up of electronic service options to fit the government's capacity to deliver high-quality services through consultation, public reporting and marketing, while assuring citizens of the government's commitment to respect their channel preferences.

- **Human resources:** developing the necessary skills in the government's workforce to adapt to change and operate effectively as a provider of client-centred services in technology-enabled, integrated, multi-channel services.

With a new governance structure in place, strategies in each of the five key areas are beginning to produce results.

Source: Canada Country Paper (2002a).

Box 29. **Spain: Catalonian government multiple service delivery channels – ".Cat"**

In 2002, the Catalonian government established a public company called ".Cat", an Internet company and a single point of contact with the government. The shareholders are the Catalonian government (the *Generalitat*) and a consortium of the 800 Catalonian local authorities. .Cat does not produce services itself, but it packages offerings from across the public sector and delivers them to citizens and businesses. Services are delivered using multiple channels enabled by a .Cat portal. The company also acts as the government's customer relationship manager, using CRM and automated workflow to measure the quality of service delivery and provide the administration with a more complete view of the citizens and businesses that it serves.

The mandate of .Cat is to simplify citizens' relationships with government by creating new channels of interaction, and then interconnecting all the channels and procedures. The .Cat portal supports all the channels which will ultimately include 200 services, information and transactions, delivered as packages based around life events. No transactions are conducted through departmental websites; all interactions between government and citizen will be through the .Cat platform. .Cat management works with government departments to establish priorities for which services to put online, and has a free hand to manage all electronic service delivery. For example .Cat has the authority to reach into each department to pull out the common components, so as to deliver them as a whole package.

Cat portal: *www.cat365.net*

Source: Holmes (2002b).

However, the following design issues and trade-offs need to be explored (Macintosh, 2002):

- Balancing the need for straightforward access to systems with the need to collect personal data for various reasons such as authentication and evaluation.
- Balancing the need for standard, generic interface features with the need to reflect the expectations of a variety of target audiences.
- Supporting easy and flexible navigation through issues.
- Deciding how much information should be provided to help individuals to be adequately informed on issues and so have the competency to contribute.

Box 30. **Japan: Guidelines for disabled accessible website contents**

In order to facilitate increased participation in government, Japan has decided that it is important to enable the disabled to access government Websites easily. The guidelines give Web content makers (homepage makers, page designers) and developers of Website tools and methods for creating barrier-free Web content that can be converted to diverse forms. The guidelines involve:

- Need for alternative means of representing content using sound and images.

- Avoidance of dependence on colour information.

- Appropriate use of mark-ups and style sheets.

- Need for clarity in the use of natural language.

- Ensuring that tables created can be converted.

- Ensuring that users can convert new technologies where necessary.

- Ensuring that pages are accessible even if users have not introduced or do not use newer technologies.

- Ensuring that users can cope with content that changes over time.

- Accessibility of the user interface.

- Ensuring that the design does not rely on specific equipment (devices).

- Emergency countermeasures should be available.

- Technical standards and guidelines for the Internet must be respected.

The guidelines for creating content that can be understood and is navigable involve:

- Providing information on context and page structures.

- Explaining clearly the system of navigation.

- Clarity and concision of documents.

Source: Guidelines prepared by the "Study Group for the Improvement of 'Information Barrier-free' Environment" (held jointly by the former Ministry of Posts and Telecommunications and the Ministry of Health and Welfare in 1998) based on the Recommendation "Web Content Accessibility Guideline 1.0" issued in May 1999 by the Web Accessibility Initiative of the World Wide Web Consortium.

- Finally, balancing rights of access, protection of privacy and security with issues of transparency, accountability and trust.

> ## Box 31.   **Italy: Ensuring accessible government websites for the disabled**
>
> The objective of this bill is to guarantee that products – typically office equipment, software and Web pages – meet the accessibility requirements of people with disabilities such as sight or hearing impairments or mobility or dexterity limitations. It requires, for the first time, the Italian public administrations' electronic information to be accessible to people with disabilities and prescribes that any new information technology that the public administration acquires should be accessible to everyone, including people with disabilities. Moreover the bill has been conceived so as to adjust to the development of all technologies that support disabled people.
>
> Finally to avoid that the bill remains just a declaration of principles, the following provisions were introduced: solicitation and contract rules for technology purchases for the public administration; a timeframe for the implementation of websites for the disabled.
>
> *Source:* OECD E-Government Working Group.

When, who and how?

The OECD report "Promises and Problems of E-Democracy: Challenges of Online Citizen Engagement" (OECD 2003b) examines a number of country case studies on e-consultation. The report raises three key questions that are rapidly emerging when approaching online engagement of citizens in policy making, namely: when? who? and how?

When? Most of the case studies in the report describe e-engagement exercises at the **agenda-setting** stage of the policy cycle. This is not surprising given that this stage of the process is most open to suggestions from citizens and is characterised by a significant degree of public deliberation, which new ICT tools are designed to facilitate. It may also indicate the exploratory or experimental nature of these online initiatives, given that this is the stage where e-engagement is most likely to complement, rather than disrupt, traditional methods of policy making. A few countries offer examples of online tools adapted for use at all stages of the policy cycle; others offer illustrations of e-engagement at a specific stage (*e.g.* policy formulation or monitoring). Whether the lack of examples of online engagement during the implementation and evaluation stages of policy making indicates that these are less amenable to e-engagement, or simply less widespread, remains an open question.

Who? The case studies illustrate the **wide range of public bodies** now exploring the use of new ICTs to engage citizens in policy making with local governments, national governments and parliaments, and bodies operating at the intergovernmental or international level (*e.g.* the European Commission). Obviously, the objectives, scope and target groups of e-engagement efforts undertaken by these bodies differ considerably. Nonetheless, they all offer valuable insights into the opportunities, dynamics and limitations of online information, consultation and participation in policy making. The target groups addressed also vary and may include all citizens (*e.g.* within a given geographic area), all interested parties (*e.g.* independently of location) or specific sub-sections of the population (*e.g.* marginalised groups, businessmen, youth).

How? Most case studies illustrate the importance of ensuring the **integration** of online and traditional methods of citizen engagement in policy making both to provide information on a policy issue or the e-engagement exercise (*e.g.* through posters, printed brochures, local press) and to offer a range of options for citizens to provide feedback (*e.g.* post, telephone, fax, e-mail or co-ordinated traditional and online discussion forums). The importance of active promotion of online consultation exercises (*e.g.* through leaflets, stickers, Website advertising banners) is also important. Specific technologies chosen for e-engagement vary in their degree of sophistication – but most feature a dedicated Website with e-mail options. Others adopt specialised software to manage online deliberations or use password-protected discussion areas for registered users. It is also essential to ensure competent and constructive moderation of online deliberations.

Access to information

The Internet is the medium of choice when providing citizens with access to government information anytime, anywhere. ICTs offer powerful tools for searching, selecting and integrating the vast amounts of information held by public administrations as well as presenting the results in a form that can be used by individual citizens.

Access to information by citizens regarding government and administrative activities remains a basic precondition of government accountability, reinforcing formal representative arrangements. This opening up of processes, whether for policy decision-making, processing of applications or government procurement can, through external scrutiny by citizens and civil society organisations, reinforce ethical behaviour and the consistent application of laws and regulations.

Online information provision can also be an important element in preventing corruption. Information on entitlements and costs of services can open up decision making and reduce opportunities for arbitrary behaviour. Systems that guide applicants through complex entitlement procedures can be incorporated into information provision and can help reduce fears of

> ### Box 32. Korea: Preventing corruption by improving transparency in administration
>
> In the past, citizens not only had to worry about unreasonable charges arising from delays for civil applications; they were also unable to track the processing of their applications. To alleviate these problems, the Internet Procedure Enhancement for Civil Applications, which provides access to information on application, processing and result of civil services through the Internet, was adopted.
>
> Currently, information on applications, review results and government employees responsible for civil applications is available on the Internet for all government organisations, including local governments and communities. (An example is the Seoul metropolitan government's OPEN system at *http://open.metro.seoul.kr*)
>
> This system has made civil administration services highly transparent by eliminating unreasonable processing of civil applications and reducing processing time.
>
> *Source:* OECD E-Government Working Group.

corruption by clarifying the decision-making process. Online tracking of the processing of an application can also be a mechanism to promote openness and reduce fears of corruption, particularly when linked to formal timeliness standards for approval processes.

Decision-support systems that guide applicants through complex processes or legislative entitlement provisions can also, through use, improve the confidence of citizens that laws and regulations are being applied fairly. This can reduce administrative and judicial appeals, which impose costs on both administrations and customers. Take-up of entitlements will also be facilitated by helping potential applicants and their advocates better understand the options available.

Government information can also be seen in broad terms as a common resource of value for a range of individual social and economic processes that, in the great majority of cases, do not involve engagement with government. The online environment provides the opportunity for government to act as an authoritative source of information, and to this end, many governments build on existing business and other information programmes. Some of the most popular government Websites deal with the weather and genealogy, hardly a major policy focus of government.

Access and *accessibility* are two key issues in enabling citizen to obtain online information, as defined in a recent report on online consultation by the Government Online International Network (Poland, 2001, p. 9):

- **Access:** "the real possibility of consulting or acquiring government information electronically".

- **Accessibility:** "the ease with which one can actually make use of the possibility of consulting government information electronically". This definition usefully emphasises the perspective of end users of government information and their capacity to find, digest and use relevant information. The report proposes seven criteria to determine the degree of accessibility of online information: recognisability and localisability; availability; manageability; affordability; reliability; clarity; and the ability to cater for special needs (*e.g.* persons with disabilities).

Improving the accessibility of online information can be achieved by: providing the information in terms of specific life events or policy issues; search engines; software for style checking and improving the intelligibility of government texts; multilingual translations of official documents; provision of online glossaries. Measures that facilitate access of **the disabled** to web-based information and the provision of information in a range of **community languages** are also necessary on equity grounds.

Consultation

The unprecedented degree of interactivity offered by ICT has the potential to expand the scope, breadth and depth of government consultations with citizens and other key stakeholders during policy making. At the same time, these new tools pose significant challenges to governments in terms of their technical, political and constitutional implications. Among the questions raised are: How can government ensure an equal hearing and assured listening to so many individual voices? How will such inputs be integrated into the policy-making cycle? What is the role of traditional mediators (such as civil society organisations) and elected representatives (such as parliamentarians)?

A number of tools are available to governments intent on collecting citizens' views and suggestions on issues proposed for online consultation, including: government consultation portals or Websites; e-mail lists; online discussion forums; online mediation systems to support deliberations; ICT support for off-line consultations. Current experience in OECD countries clearly shows the importance of ensuring competent, independent and effective moderation of online public deliberations.

In the interests of transparency and accountability, governments also need to develop ICT-supported tools for the analysis of public input and to provide feedback to citizens on how their comments and suggestions have been used in reaching decisions on public policy.

Among the issues to be addressed when launching online consultations are (Macintosh, 2002):

- Who defines the criteria by which citizens' inputs are analysed?
- How can e-contributions be incorporated into decision-making?
- How are judgements made about the relative weight of e-contributions with respect to other inputs?
- How and to what extent can technology support or highlight areas of agreement and disagreement?
- Can technology adequately support the summarising and content analysis of contributions?

As has long been the case in traditional off-line consultations, the earlier e-consultation takes place in the policy cycle the better its chances. Online consultation also faces some specific challenges, such as its in-built self-selection of participants with access to the Internet; this raises the risk of over-representation of a small cross-section of the population. However, such risks can be obviated by efforts to enable wider access (through public kiosks, cyber-cafes and community centres, as well as TV and other digital platforms) and an adequate investment by government in promoting and supporting online consultations.

Public participation

As defined in the OECD's *Citizens as Partners* (2001e), active citizen participation in policy making is "a relationship based on partnership with government in which citizens actively engage in defining the process and content of policy-making. It acknowledges equal standing for citizens in setting the agenda, proposing policy options and shaping the policy dialogue – although the responsibility for the final decision or policy formulation rests with government" (Citizens as Partners, OECD 2001e). Few concrete examples of this strong formulation of government-citizen partnership are to be found at national level, whether online or off-line.

Options for online public participation are currently being explored in OECD countries. They include the use of e-petitions (to government or parliament); online referendums and shared online work spaces for deliberations and development of policy options. Additionally citizen participation includes proactive engagement in the provision of public services, such as community-based activities.

Only a very few OECD countries, however, have begun to experiment with online tools and discussion formats that leave citizens much latitude for proposing opportunities for participation, setting the agenda for discussion, submitting their own proposals and shaping the final outcomes (OECD, 2001, p. 58). While many of the barriers to innovative forms of e-engagement may be technical, others are more closely related to cultural resistance in policy making to new forms of partnership with citizens and civil society and factors that shape the traditional policy process in representative democracies.

Future challenges

The main challenges for e-engagement include (Macintosh, 2002):

- **Scale.** From a citizen's perspective, the question is how technology can ensure that an individual's voice is not lost in a broad debate. One approach is to design technology to give individuals the electronic means to find others with a similar point of view. There is a need for technology to make available virtual public spaces in which an individual's voice can develop into a community (public) voice. From a government perspective, there is the challenge of how to listen to and respond to every individual. Fostering online communities and developing e-engagement tools to support such communities could enable a more collective approach.

- **Capacity.** The second challenge is harnessing ICTs to encourage citizens to think constructively about public issues and listen to, and engage in, argument and counter-argument. There is therefore a need for accessible and understandable information and an opportunity to debate using tools such as next-generation mediated discussion forums. Related to this challenge is the effort to involve otherwise disenfranchised groups in policy making (e.g. the socially excluded, youth). There is a need for e-engagement tools that provide citizens with an opportunity to participate in, and to understand, collective decision making and develop the skills of active citizenship.

- **Coherence.** Governments need to take a holistic view of the policy-making cycle and design technology to support the processes of informing, consulting, participating, analysing, providing feedback and evaluating. Inputs received at each stage in the policy-making cycle need to be made available at other stages of the process so that policy is better formulated and citizens are better informed. Consideration should be given to addressing if, and to what extent, knowledge management techniques can support the policy-making cycle.

- **Learning.** Online engagement in policy making is new and examples of good practice are scarce, hence the need to build on the experience of others and the need for comparative work. National governments should take advantage of innovative e-engagement work under way at the local level, in parliaments and in other countries. Of course, any e-engagement system that proves successful in a given context must be adapted to the culture, traditions and objectives of other government units that might wish to replicate their experience.

- **Evaluation.** Tools are needed to assess what value added online engagement has, or has not, brought to policy making. There is a need to understand how to assess the benefits and the impacts of applying technology to open up the policy process to wider public input. As governments increasingly support the development of ICTs to enable citizen engagement on policy-related matters, there is a corresponding need to know whether e-engagement meets both governments' and citizens' objectives (see also section on Monitoring and Evaluation).

4.3. Back office

The term "back office" refers to the internal operations of an organisation that support core processes and are not accessible or visible to the general public. The implementation of e-government goes hand-in-hand with a number of back office reforms. On the one hand e-government will help bring about these reforms, while on the other hand e-government requires such reforms in order to be successful. The back-office operations described in this Chapter include:

- Organisational Change.
- Leadership.
- Central co-ordination.
- Collaboration.
- Ensuring skills.
- Public-private partnerships.
- Managing risk and cost.
- Monitoring and Evaluation.

In this Chapter, each of these areas will be discussed in turn.

Organisational change

ICTs have been changing the way public administrations operate since they were first introduced in the 1950s and 1960s. ICT influences both overall efficiency and organisational change as it increases the capacity to implement work flexibility, provides tools for more effective and collaborative decision-making and service delivery, and creates opportunities for rethinking traditional business processes.

The use of ICT has an impact on operations efficiency by transforming mass as well as internal business processing tasks such as personnel record keeping and payments to officials and contractors. Further savings may accrue from benefits of scale, for example, in the case of e-procurement and from reduced corruption when ICTs are used to promote transparency. In the government environment, however, while a specific process may be improved, **productivity gains may not result in programme savings**. The bulk of savings due to process improvements generally come from a reduction in staff resources, as routine tasks are automated. However it may not actually be possible to actually reduce staff numbers. In such cases, efficiencies gained from improving a routine process may be reallocated to enhance service quality by freeing staff no longer required for routine processing to provide more individual assistance to those with more complex problems.

The introduction of ICT into the public workplace also requires accompanying process changes in order to make the most of e-government. All too often, ICTs are overlaid on an existing organisational structure without any thought to how those structures can be improved. Governments have tended to use technology as a patch to provide a seamless interface with users to a complex administrative structure. The creation of national portals, for example, has often consisted of the rearrangement of existing information without implying a fundamental change in processes and procedures or the creation of collaborative frameworks. Within agencies, incentives for greater information sharing and collaboration would help the implementation of organisational change.

Introducing ICT has created opportunities to rethink organisational processes for improving service delivery. Evidence from both private and public sectors reinforces the view that ICT needs to be seen as one aspect of a reform package that allows organisations to achieve greater efficiency and other governance objectives. Member countries understand the need for a series of changes, involving both ICT and non-ICT elements. The benefits sought – more effective outputs, greater efficiency – require more than just introducing ICT into existing organisations and work processes.

ICT can foster the adoption of new organisational practices through increased interactions and information sharing. This has had an impact both on the use of ICT to perform tasks within government, but also more broadly on the expectations and working habits of a new generation growing up in the information society. While efforts are only now beginning to look at the long-term impact of these changes, many expect that improved communications will lead to flattened hierarchies and increasingly networked and collaborative work models.

For e-government to deliver benefits, the ways in which public administrations work will have to change. This process has already begun. This section of the report looks at the broad organisational changes that are needed

THE E-GOVERNMENT IMPERATIVE – ISBN 92-64-10117-9 – © OECD 2003

to build sustainable change around e-government and at organisational features that may be emerging in response to the rollout of e-government initiatives.

Types of organisational change

Small-scale ICT activity, such as the development of a Website as an additional publication and service channel, may not initially require complex supporting changes. However in the long-term this will require far reaching organisational change, especially as websites begin to offer deeper, more complex types of services.

The challenge of providing seamless services entails a certain blurring of roles and functions within the administration as organisations are asked to work together to deliver services according to the needs of citizen and business and not their own internal structures. The necessary sharing of information and tasks makes it much more difficult to ensure internal accountability within the public administration. While the need for checking or direct supervision of achievement of individual tasks may diminish, new challenges will emerge such as the performance management of teams within and across agencies, the prevention of abuses arising from shared data and the motivation of individuals who are either tele-working or part of virtual teams.

Re-engineering processes may require a shift in the balance of roles and responsibilities between different functional areas or between the agency's central office and local offices. Increased data sharing within an organisation may upset individual arrangements, by making particular data holdings (and their operators) redundant, and require concerted management effort to gain acceptance of the new arrangements. Greater sharing of data, enhanced communication and more consistent decision making can facilitate a devolution of decision making to an organisation's lower levels. It can also foster either the creation of specialised units at local level or of units focused on specific customer groups, while maintaining overall policy coherence.

From a government-wide perspective, organisational change is needed to harmonise working processes and to improve co-ordination and collaboration between organisations. Effective service delivery requires different organisational units across government to be able to interact and co-operate efficiently. Cross-government projects, involving different agencies, should be based on knowledge sharing and led by agency experts willing to share expertise.

Internal resistance to change

To date, government structures have been resilient in the face of technological change. Traditional bureaucracies still hold sway in public administrations, albeit in an environment of reform that has seen greater use of devolved agencies, the elimination or outsourcing of non-core activities and increasing performance flexibility for public administration managers.

When planning organisational change, two basic issues need to be addressed: the willingness and ability to adopt new ways of working and the need for understanding and support by senior management. Internal resistance may prevent the adoption of the workplace practices necessary to make the best use of ICT.

Within agencies, successful e-government requires helping government employees to understand their role and expectations as part of ICT-enabled processes. Introducing successful reform requires coherent change management strategies. For example, new work processes need to be accompanied by job redesign, training programmes and structured

---

Box 33.   **Canada: Creating an agile work force within existing and evolving structures**

The public expects governments to provide high-quality service across all channels, including the Internet, and to use the most effective practices and technologies. Meeting these expectations requires a more agile workforce capable of adapting government processes rapidly in response to changing needs and circumstances. This involves fundamental changes in cultures and a commitment to creating "learning organisations".

The Organisational Readiness Office in the Chief Information Officer Branch of the Treasury Board of Canada Secretariat has adopted a community-based strategy to address human resource issues related to service transformation in the information technology, information management and service delivery communities. Members of these communities are public servants who play strategically crucial roles in transforming and "e-enabling" service delivery.

Community-led initiatives such as competency-based staffing, greater use of pre-qualified pools, generic competitions for executive-level positions, repositories of work descriptions and the e-Learning Gateway are demonstrating that existing legislation and regulations are not insurmountable barriers to the modern management practices needed to implement a service transformation agenda.

Source: Fine (2002).

communications strategies. Establishing ownership of reforms can also keep employees from attempting to bypass organisational reforms by replicating traditional processes informally. Dialogue with stakeholders both within and outside the organisation is an important element for success.

As with the introduction of e-government across the whole of government, support from senior management is a pre-condition for successful organisational change. This requires more than statements of principle and good intentions. Crucially, it involves senior management time and understanding, factors which can be in short supply. Examples of successful major reforms involving ICTs indicate that senior management's understanding of the impacts of proposed reforms and their risks and benefits, is required if the reforms are to be sold to staff and to key external stakeholders such as political leaders. Such a commitment provides assurance that actions will be consistent with rhetoric.

High-level commitment will be determined by the willingness of senior management to commence the process of changing the organisational culture by adopting new ways of working. It will also depend on the willingness and ability of unions and individual staff to adopt new work practices, such as more decentralised decision making, teamwork, information sharing among peers, new recruitment arrangements and remuneration and incentives to support the desired changes.

Challenges

OECD analysis of the use of ICTs by firms has highlighted the importance of flexible labour markets and the legal frameworks covering ICT-based activity and the need generally to reduce barriers to initiative and innovation (Murphy 2002). While governments need to balance a full range of factors, public administration frameworks will need to allow ministries and agencies to adopt new practices arising from e-government.

In order to achieve a sustainable organisational change, public governance frameworks should be improved. While frameworks differ greatly across OECD member countries, key aspects are likely to include the following:

Human resource management policies should allow for flexible remuneration and working conditions, for the development of teams, for performance management in the context of virtual and/or cross organisational teams, for flexible working hours to deal with demand peaks and for job redesign to cover a broad range of customer needs and government programmes.

Legal frameworks should provide public officials with certainty regarding their use of ICTs, for example regarding liability for advice provided online, the status of electronic decision- making processes, of authentication and of online business processes.

Privacy and data protection frameworks should clarify the situation as regards the sharing of information within and between agencies, officials' rights and responsibilities, and the rights and entitlements of citizens.

On the basis of the foregoing, some tentative conclusions can be drawn:

- Government use of ICT should be seen as an enabler rather than as an end in itself, with the objective of facilitating the achievement of policy and business goals. ICT use will thus be driven on a case-by-case basis, according to specific requirements and objectives. The resulting shape and operation of specific organisations will **reflect particular applications** and the changes adopted to carry out their functions and achieve their objectives.

- The incorporation of new technologies will be an **ongoing process**, reflecting new technological developments and the maturing of existing technologies to the stage where they can be applied in an operational government context. While the current focus is on the Internet, and its current functionality, this is a dynamic process, albeit with phases of different rates of development and change.

- While individual processes may be transformed, changes will occur less quickly for organisations. The larger and more complicated the organisation, the longer it will take. For public administrations overall, the rate of change will be slower still.

- While certain ways of working may become more pervasive in the future, with greater data sharing and networking, greater process automation and greater collaboration among and within agencies, there will be **no single model** for e-government organisations. Even if there were, it would soon be out of date.

- Those dealing with public management organisational issues should act as **facilitators** rather than developing grand plans to restructure public administrations around technologies. Frameworks are required for ICT use, and they need to be reviewed to ensure their continuing relevance. Broader internal governance frameworks for public administration need to be reviewed to ensure that they support, rather than hinder, the adoption of ICT-enabled reforms.

- Senior management commitment is essential for carrying out complex organisational changes. Major changes are disruptive by definition and in particular may raise broad managerial and political issues that go beyond the organisation involved. Dealing with potential job losses as a result of ICT initiatives is particularly challenging. E-government co-ordinators can provide support to senior managers by ensuring the sharing of experiences and good practice approaches (see section on leadership).

- The involvement of front-line staff at the project initiation stage is increasingly seen as an effective way of reducing the conception-reality gap between the initiation of reform projects and final deliverables.

Leadership

E-government implementation can be difficult, risky and expensive. Governments are increasingly asked to translate a general vision into effective public services while facing time constraints, lack of resources and political pressures. The cost of losing the reform momentum can be high.

Leadership is not just about motivating people and creating incentives and opportunities for actions. E-government is also about change, and many e-government advances to date have been driven by the enthusiasm of individuals and individual agencies. But there can be considerable resistance to change particularly to the level of change required if some of the more significant efficiencies and service enhancements through seamless online services are to be realised. While the form and arrangements adopted will be very much determined in the context of each member country's political and administrative environment, and will continue to evolve as lessons are learnt, leadership is an essential ingredient of e-government in order to **motivate and break down barriers to change**.

Sustained leadership is important at all levels of the e-government cycle. At the early stages, there is a need to gain acceptance of concepts and benefits, and to put in place frameworks to sustain momentum and structure implementation in an efficient manner. As more complex transactional services are implemented, the need for leadership and support will continue, particularly as benefits may take time to emerge.

Leadership is a catalyst for innovation. Broad reforms require perspectives and pioneers able to translate the vision into action. E-government leaders should learn how to put in place the right administrative mechanism to support agencies in the e-government implementation.

Types of leadership

There are many styles of leadership. Different kinds of leadership may co-exist and be a key to success, depending on the stage of the e-government process. In a very early stage of e-government development the leader may obtain views on what needs to change, share a common vision with the personnel and evaluate new ideas. In a more mature stage, selling the benefits of a vision and creating personnel commitment to it are required.

Leadership can be exercised at **all levels of the organisation**. Political leadership has an important role in shaping and backing e-government initiatives. Political leaders contribute to the establishment of the e-government

> ## Box 34. **Estonia: Mobilising with a unifying concept and presidential leadership**
>
> Presidential leadership in Estonia declared Internet access a human right, thus creating strong national support for the implementation of the Tiger Leap Forward Initiative, a multi-sector programme with the overall objective to create an e-society. The Estonian President was an outspoken advocate for the Internet, and this greatly influenced the success of the initiative.
>
> The concept of the Tiger Leap was initiated at a high political level, when Ambassador of Estonia to the US and the Minister of Education initiated an exchange in 1996. This exchange was based on the idea that the new information and communication technology will alter not only the general life arrangement but the whole educational paradigm. Symbolising the radical changes and technological spurt proposed for Estonia, the programme was called Tiger Leap upon the example of the economic giants in Asia.
>
> The programme was defined to include participation of the President of Estonia as patron of the programme. On February 21, 1996 the President declared the Tiger Leap project officially open in his address on the national television.
>
> The Tiger Leap project has been successful, in part because of strong, high-level leadership:
>
> - A key feature of Tiger Leap was a commitment to connect every school in Estonia to the Internet, a goal that was achieved in 2000. The Foundation is currently giving support to about 720 primary and secondary schools, including about 100 schools that serve the Russian-speaking minority in Estonia.
>
> - As a result of these efforts, the generation of Estonians now in school are 100% computer literate. Teachers report that students are highly motivated to learn computing, both out of personal interest and because they know it will lead to better job opportunities.
>
> - Tiger Leap has also had an impact in publicising the Internet: the media attention given to the programme ensured that Estonians heard about the Internet even if they had never used it themselves, and it reinforced the feeling that Internet access was something important.
>
> *Source:* The Tiger Leap Foundation.

vision, define priorities, filter citizens' needs, make the decisions and provide the will to carry them out. Strong political leadership can make a difference in forcing the momentum for change and easing the reform process. It can also increase management motivation and sense of responsibility.

THE E-GOVERNMENT IMPERATIVE – ISBN 92-64-10117-9 – © OECD 2003

Box 35. **Korea: the role of the leadership in e-government**

Until recently, individual ministries in Korea had carried out the implementation of e-government without any co-ordination among departments. After an initial phase of uncertainty due to internal resistance to change, a non-standing committee with both government and non-government members was created and co-chaired by a civilian member and the Senior Secretary to the President for Policy and Planning. The committee met the requirements of ministries, in particular the Ministry of Information and Communication and the Ministry of Government Administration and Home Affairs who had previously debated its optimal structure.

The committee became the key e-government co-ordinating body. The committee's ability to bring about inter-departmental co-operation largely depended on the leadership role of the President, the powers afforded it to co-ordinate between ministries, the personal networks of the committee members and the goodwill and integrity of members. Its non-threatening status and overarching role facilitated early progress, which also led to greater respect and participation from ministries.

In Korea, high-level leadership has enabled the committee to stand above ministerial conflicts and promote an environment of co-operation better than if it was headed by a particular ministry or even jointly between two or more ministries. At the same time it stresses the role of the President as an active leader with a strong interest in backing the government initiative and to push for achieving greater co-ordination. The personal and professional ties of the chairmen formed over the years have served as a tool in building a strong network for the committee and linking government with various sources that further enhanced capacity to create e-government.

Source: Korea Country Paper (2002a).

Leadership can also articulate a unifying theme that can propel the e-government initiative through all the necessary steps. It is important to understand that results are most likely when leaders elevate the public profile of their vision and press for its successful implementation by tying it to broader government policy agendas.

Political leadership is also linked to administrative simplicity. As a tool for administrative process simplification, e-government can be used as an effective reform leverage only if there is a strong political leadership to support its introduction and development.

Ministerial level involvement is essential to ensure vertical e-government planning, to get the necessary resources, to motivate staff and support

> ### Box 36. Finland: Lower-management leadership
>
> Interviews with several Finnish ministries and agencies that were advanced in terms of e-government planning and implementation gave the impression that top management interest in and support of e-government activities were not present at the outset. The main drivers of e-government initiatives were the need to make organisational changes and awareness by lower-level managers that e-government could be used to support changes in the business process. Given the proper initiative (and resources), IT offices can drive change. An IT official from the Ministry of Labour said, "saying that it is the fault of the political authorities not getting involved is an easy way out".
>
> This is not to say that top management responsibility is not important when planning e-government. What is suggested instead, is that extensive e-government planning and implementation can succeed in launching e-government without top management involvement if an organisation has extremely innovative lower-level managers and e-government initiatives which can facilitate general organisational changes.
>
> *Source:* OECD report on E-Government in Finland (2003).

dealings with external partners and stakeholders and to ensure co-operation across ministries and agencies. Such management involvement, support and responsibility is also necessary in order to produce an e-strategy that is integrated both with the general business plan of the organisation as well as incorporated into the planning and budget process. Senior management attention, however, is a scarce resource and ICT projects are often regarded as low priority technical issues rather then key to the success of the overall business plan (see The Hidden Threat to E-Government, OECD, 2001).

Top management initiatives to drive organisational changes should be accompanied by efforts at all levels of management. E-government planning and implementation requires not just top management involvement but innovative lower level managers, able to translate a broad e-government vision or objectives into precise actions and policies.

Leadership as a co-ordination tool

Leadership is an indispensable tool to promote co-ordination within the organisation, and is fundamental in managing e-government projects. This is even more important in the public sector where governments have a wider mix in their products and services than have private companies making co-ordination even harder. Managers must be able to exercise leadership and to manage responsibilities of their own IT systems.

> ## Box 37. Japan: The IT Strategy Headquarters
>
> The Japanese government has recently undertaken significant efforts in promoting the development of the information society, with e-government playing the role of the catalyst for IT spread. The political and governmental support to the project has been essential in setting up the organisational structures.
>
> In January 2001, the "Strategy Headquarters for the Promotion of an Advanced Information and Telecommunications Network Society" (the IT Strategy Headquarters) was established within the Cabinet for the purpose of "further promoting policy measures rapidly and intensively to create an advanced information and telecommunications network society".
>
> The Headquarters is chaired by the Prime Minister and consists of all the Cabinet ministers, representatives from the private sector, etc. It is in charge of formulating and adopting overall national IT strategies and policies, e-government being one of the major issues dealt with by the Headquarters.
>
> A body in charge of IT policy had existed within the cabinet ever since 1994, but the new Headquarters differs in that: 1) it was established by the strong leadership of the Prime Minister; 2) a law was adopted in the *Diet* for its foundation and, therefore, it has explicit duties and powers; 3) it has its own secretariat with exclusive staff.
>
> The IT Strategy Headquarters adopted the most important IT and e-government strategic documents ("e-Japan Strategy" in January 2001, the "e-Japan Priority Policy Program" in March 2001, the "e-Japan 2002 Programme in June 2001, the "Acceleration and Advancement of the e-Japan Priority Policy Program and the e-Japan 2002 Program" in November 2001 and the "e-Japan Priority Policy Program 2002" in June 2002).
>
> The IT Strategic Headquarters reviews the priority policy programme every spring, studies the implementation status of measures every spring and autumn, and make the study results public, in order to ensure steady implementation of the measures included in the programme.
>
> *Source:* Japan Country Paper (2002a).

Leadership is not about centralisation of competencies. In an increasingly complex environment, e-government organisation should be in line with the principles of delegation of power and responsibilities. Creating local leaders (team leaders, project leaders, etc.) is a key answer to the principle of decentralised management and decision power over IT in their own organisation.

As e-government disrupts old organisational hierarchies and facilitates team working and information sharing, the ability to co-ordinate people, resources and responsibilities may become an asset. Japan's experience revealed how strong leadership from their Prime Minister strengthened executive level co-ordination by facilitating e-government strategies and policies among ministries (see box, above).

Challenges to e-government leadership

Exercising leadership implies knowing an organisation's strengths and weaknesses and being able to make the organisation commit to the achievement of goals even if this can lead to the breaking of internal balance and distribution of power. In order to foster leadership and commitment, e-government initiatives should include incentives for leaders to emerge by setting up transparent organisational structures and clear sets of responsibilities.

Leadership requires certain skills, which may not be available without specific skill acquisition policies. Organisations must pay more attention to developing new leaders by improving their managerial skills and avoid thinking that structure and technology alone can supplement human resource management.

Box 38. **Principles for successful e-government leadership**

- Co-ordinating resources and responsibilities within the organisation.

- Developing a common vision and set objectives (e-agenda).

- Developing the ability to persuade people to that vision in order to convince the enthusiasts and engage the sceptics.

- Developing a customer-led and customer-focused approach.

- Ensuring that leadership can be recognised and encouraged wherever it is found in the organisation.

- Raising the awareness and developing the skills of employees, encouraging innovative solutions to organisational problems.

- Assessing and building the capacity to deliver online services, leading people through the difficult process of change, securing the commitment from staff along the way and managing their programme of work.

- Ensuring technological development within the organisation and make sure that personnel can fully benefits from that.

- Recognising the full use of technologies but not chasing technological solutions in itself.

Source: Elaborated from the Skills Foresight Report (*www.lgemployers.gov.uk/psd/eskills/leadership.htm*).

Central co-ordination

Central co-ordination is a feature of most OECD e-government strategies, and generally involves formal organisational units located within the public administration or linked to broader information society units. Central co-ordination can bring strategies from different agencies together, ensure compatibility and reduce duplication.

Benefits of central co-ordination

An important role of such central co-ordinating units is to act as a **focal point** for promoting government-wide e-government development. This may involve being responsible for developing the e-government strategy, monitoring progress towards goals, promoting benefits to the public, linking e-government activity to broader reform and information society goals and generally acting to generate and sustain momentum. This may also involve reporting on progress and reassessing strategies in the light of experience and as progress is made.

Central co-ordination can also facilitate the efficient implementation of e-government, for example by:

- Promoting **sharing of information and good practice**. Measures here include central online registers of projects, seminars, publications and Websites on good practice and communities of interest. This can also include brokering joint operating arrangements and exchange of best practice on common operating processes such as Enterprise Resource Planning systems.

- Facilitating efficient **acquisition** of ICT products and services. This may cover e-procurement, compulsory central purchasing of communications services and software, sharing of price and other information between agencies.

- Gaining acceptance across government of various **frameworks and standards** to facilitate interoperability and efficiencies, such as policy frameworks, outlining principles governing acquisition of ICT, business and technical policies and standards.

- Taking steps to avoid **duplication** of effort by information sharing, expenditure approval processes, brokering of joint contracts.

- Facilitate **collaboration** (see next section), especially regarding seamless online services and shared infrastructure projects.

Central co-ordination can also promote **innovation and risk taking**. Agencies implementing critical applications generally have little scope to experiment and take risks. If funding is available, a central e-government unit can act as a central R&D unit on behalf of agencies across government.

Invariably, some form of governance arrangements such as a co-ordination committee (or committees) have been established to develop and co-ordinate these practices. These generally comprise representatives of key agencies and may include representatives from the private sector and other levels of government.

Whole-of-government structures are important to steer e-government implementation across government, to provide a framework for collaboration across agencies and a vehicle for input from the senior management level, and to keep e-government activity aligned on broader public administration agendas. Approaches that have been adopted include committees of agency heads and chief information officers. The roles of such bodies vary, from purely advisory and information sharing, through to policy development and implementation oversight. The involvement of non-government representatives from industry bodies, academia and civil society organisations has been effective.

Box 39. **Mexico: Senior level committees**

The Mexican government has established networks of senior managers working on different topics, such as innovation, human resource management, social communication and ICT use. The latter network is formed by 60 agency chief information officers. Its goals are to build a government-wide technological infrastructure, to agree on standards, architectures and joined-up online services, to foster savings and re-engineering through ICT, to promote knowledge management and e-learning within government and to enhance citizen participation.

Source: OECD E-Government Working Group.

Requirements for co-ordination

OECD countries understand that **decentralisation** is an effective management tool. Business unit managers need to manage ICT as they do other resources and are generally the best placed to be aware of business needs that can be efficiently addressed by ICT applications. However, agencies cannot operate in isolation, especially with regard to ICT. The nature of e-government requires a level of co-operative action to ensure interoperability, avoid duplication, ensure coherent action in a range of crucial areas such as security and privacy protection, and to provide the framework and capacity for seamless services. The need for co-ordination becomes more pressing as member countries increasingly move to implement more complex, transactional services. The cost of introducing such services, and the cost of making them interoperable after they have been introduced, makes avoiding duplication and implementing projects in a structured environment all the more pressing.

There is as a result a **central dilemma** for e-government implementation. In the terms of the Finnish Council of Ministers: "a basic problem is how agencies' responsibility for results and autonomous operation can be retained while at the same time ensuring the interests of the government administration at large in questions pertaining to interoperable systems and

---

Box 40. **Italy: Network of regional competence centres (RCCs)**

The Department for Innovation Technologies in cooperation with the Department for Public Administration launched at the beginning of 2002 a nation-wide network of regional competence centres (RCCs) for the development of e-government and the information society.

The general objectives of the RCC project are: 1) to support regional and local actors in defining and implementing e-government programmes and projects, while ensuring coherence with the national strategy; 2) to identify and develop models, approaches and tools jointly to address aspects of e-government construction; and 3) to promote and support collaboration among the different levels of government within and across regions.

The RCCs are to act as facilitators. At the same time they are expected to receive, understand and co-ordinate the demands and needs of local administrations and to propose methodologies, processes and solutions. The creation of the RCCs is not imposed by central government but comes from the needs and interests of the local authorities. A strong commitment by regional and local authorities is considered essential to ensure the centre's self-sustainability after the start-up phase supported through central funds. Consequently, the RCCs are being developed at different rates in different regions.

Generally an RCC is made up of a dedicated group of four or five volunteers from different levels of government. To these groups of civil servants two to three consultants are assigned on a full-time basis by the central unit co-ordinating the project. Their role is mainly to provide technical assistance and training to local authorities that are implementing e-government projects. A central steering group ensures the circulation of ideas and practices, leading to shared features, operational approaches and service quality levels.

Source: OECD E-Government Working Group.

---

shared use of information resources". While this reflects the broader issue for government of co-ordination *versus* devolved management responsibility, if e-government is to succeed it is crucial to get the balance right. The stronger the control exercised over co-ordination, the higher the costs due to the web of regulations and requirements to which new, creative initiatives must adhere. Co-ordination may stifle innovation and initiative, leading to foregone opportunities. However a co-ordinated approach may generate efficiencies, reduce risk and facilitate a faster and broader rollout of e-government initiatives.

Peer review of anticipated projects by a panel of agencies can provide a valuable means of bringing input to the planning of the specific project. It can also provide a return to the reviewing agencies in the form of further knowledge of what is occurring across government and sharing the knowledge of peers.

Box 41. **Ireland: Peer review**

To ensure co-ordination and implementation of the e-government agenda across all departments and public agencies, a series of instruments has been put in place. A high-level cross-departmental group of senior officials (Assistant Secretaries from the Information Society Implementation Group) promotes and monitors the e-government process across the Irish public sector.

Source: Irish country submission.

Whole-of-government business and technical architectures provide a structured approach in which agencies can plan their activity, provide for interoperability across government and capture efficiencies through sharing of knowledge and joint projects. Specific information management standards support interoperability and provide users with a common interface when accessing online portals and services. Mandated minimum security, privacy and authentication standards are common. Such standards could usefully be adopted by other levels of government, such as provinces and municipalities.

One example of central co-ordination has been the use of centralised **e-procurement** systems. E-procurement is the procurement of goods through an Internet or ICT-based process. In the broadest sense, it begins with contract establishment, but also covers ordering, invoicing and payment. Efficiency needs are a driving force for e-procurement. E-procurement can lead to savings through administrative simplification and time saving, but also through increased transparency and competition among suppliers.

THE E-GOVERNMENT IMPERATIVE – ISBN 92-64-10117-9 – © OECD 2003

> ### Box 42. **Germany: SAGA – Standards and architecture for e-government applications**
>
> The German government has begun to consolidate government wide standards and guidance into one document, SAGA. SAGA has guided the implementation of e-government in Germany. Its aim is to develop standards for the smooth flow of digital information between citizens, business and the federal administration and to make as many electronic services as possible available using uniform procedures. Data models must be defined in order to develop integrated and interdisciplinary e-government applications.
>
> In its current version, SAGA can be accessed and downloaded in English at the portal of the Federal Government's Coordination and Advisory Board for IT in the Administration (KBSt) *www.kbst.bund.de/sage*. The document includes an explanation of what is necessary to respect its aims in terms of standards and architecture. SAGA describes its aims and the basic agreements, responsibilities and applications of SAGA, the architectural building blocks of SAGA, *i.e.* the components needed for a functioning e-government architecture, and the standards for the basic components defined in BundOnline 2005 (*e.g.* content management system, platform for payment transactions).
>
> SAGA is not a final document. It is constantly revised to include the latest developments and amendments. To develop the SAGA document in a targeted way, the federal government's service portal now includes a technology forum at *http://foren.kbst.bund.de*. It offers German-speaking experts and anyone interested a discussion area covering the various topics of SAGA, such as appropriate interface connections or interdisciplinary data models.
>
> *Source:* OECD E-Government Working Group.

Use of co-ordinated **budget funding** for e-government initiatives, including specific approval arrangements, can avoid duplication and help governments set priorities across overall e-government activities. However, this may also add an extra layer of regulation and absorb much senior management time and capacity. The rules by which such arrangements operate need to be clear to all parties if they are to operate effectively.

A programme of key projects can be managed to test innovative approaches, provide broader demonstration effects, provide seed funding for initiatives that remove a bottleneck, or provide a model of common processes that can be adopted by a number of agencies. Such a programme can have important longer-term benefits by encouraging agency investment that would otherwise not occur and speeding up overall progress.

Box 43. **Australia: Business authentication framework (BAF)**

Jointly managed by the Australian Taxation Office (ATO) and the Department of Employment and Workplace Relations (DEWR), in consultation with the National Office of Information Economy (NOIE), the BAF project aims at developing functionality that will allow Commonwealth government agencies to authenticate the online identity of businesses that use the agencies' e-commerce applications. The BAF provides utilities to assist agencies with the development of e-commerce applications using public key infrastructure (a Certificate Signing Interface – CSI) and will assist with the validation of incoming business certificates by providing a centralised validation service (Certificate Validation System – CVS).

The BAF collaboration grew out of a number of business-centred e-commerce initiatives undertaken by the ATO and DEWR which require digital signature certificates as core enablers for secure and trusted messages sent via the Internet. While each agency is nominally responsible for developing one project element (i.e. the CSI element by the ATO and the CVS by the DEWR), which suggests a straightforward division of labour, the success of the project nonetheless depends on the mutual dependency of the two elements and requires close collaboration for the BAF project as a whole.

The BAF Joint Taskforce was established to manage the development and implementation of both elements of the framework, and is represented by ATO, DEWR and NOIE. It has two main groups.

- A senior executives group meets periodically to manage high-level issues, including the impact and influence of the BAF on other initiatives. The group includes representatives from other agencies that might use the BAF, such as the Australian Customs Service.

- A project management group, whose more direct role is to steer the BAF project to the completion of specific milestones.

There is also an associated users group, with members from interested government agencies and businesses. Owing to successful collaboration between the two agencies through the joint taskforce, and the structure of the taskforce itself, the BAF is now approaching operational readiness. The CSI recently entered a testing phase, and the CVS is due to begin testing soon.

Source: OECD E-Government Working Group.

For the above measures to operate effectively, they require:

- **Central resources and support from the e-government co-ordinating agency or a lead agency.** For example, structured information sharing arrangements require at least some support to operate effectively and to

> ## Box 44. **World leaders in e-procurement**
>
> The Interchange of Data between Administrations (IDA) Transborder eProcurement Study identified the world leaders in e-procurement to be: Australia, Canada, Finland, Germany, Norway, the United Kingdom and the United States. These countries have clear and nationally defined e-procurement strategies, and a wide range of mature projects in place.
>
> The report especially mentioned Finland as "the most advanced system", as it covers almost all of the procurement cycle. However, the OECD Report on E-Government in Finland found that the Finnish central e-procurement system only handles about 3-4% of Finland's total government purchases.
>
> Source: IDA 2002 and the OECD Report on E-Government on Finland.

remain valuable. Specific arrangements need to be reviewed over time to remain relevant and to take advantage of new approaches.

● Commitment by participating agencies. At the simplest, this will involve a commitment of staff time, for example, to release qualified staff to review activities and to participate in policy development committees.

● **A government framework that acknowledges the value of co-ordination.** Government-endorsed e-government policies generally provide the overall context, but the message needs to be reinforced, at both the political and senior public management level, that such co-ordination is valuable and indeed essential for many aspects of e-government activity. A particular target group is agency leaders, who, understandably, are driven by urgent agency-specific agendas, and need to see the value of devoting resources to co-ordination and shared information, with short-term costs and less apparent longer-term benefits. Engaging this group is extremely important.

● **In a number of areas, such as security, privacy and authentication, minimum standards must apply to all agencies.** These are generally embodied in legislation or regulations. The greater the degree of compulsion, the greater the responsibility on e-government co-ordinating agencies to make correct judgements and to involve user agencies in the decision. Consultation with user agencies to develop and implement requirements will be crucial.

These efforts can provide a framework for the efficient rollout of e-government initiatives. Requirements to share information on anticipated projects will help avoid duplication of spending and facilitate better use of corporate knowledge.

Given the inherently decentralised nature of e-government implementation, such an approach implies a model that is more co-operative and horizontal than a top-down framework controlled by a central co-ordinating agency. In such a context, the latter's role is broadly to facilitate sharing among agencies; ensuring that the overall regulatory framework is efficient; and managing whole-of-government key projects, frameworks and functions (see below).

Collaboration and seamless services

The dominant structural forms in all OECD governments are "stovepipe" or "silo" organisational units. Such units have relatively clear, mutually exclusive areas of responsibility and control and political accountability. However, the capacity to offer integrated, seamless government services so that users can interact with government as a single organisation, represents one of the major advantages of Internet and broad ICT use in government.

The development of a customer focus requires collaboration. One-stop shops, advice bureaux, whole-of-government telephone call centres and services such as information kiosks have attempted to bring together information and services from different government agencies.

The Internet has brought a quantum leap in efforts to provide this customer focus, and member countries are actively developing initiatives to draw together information and services for specific customer groups. These seamless online services aim to transcend the agency-based structure of the supply of information and services and present users with a coherent, integrated package of government information and services. Such services can provide higher levels of value to customers than separate services.

As services become more complex, efficiency considerations require greater co-operation between agencies, in areas such as authentication, shared processing and the exchange of data. The need for collaboration between agencies thus has both "front-office" (service to the customer) and "back-office" (efficiency in government) dimensions. From the customer's point of view, government should appear as one organisation; from government agencies' point of view, the customer should appear as a single customer.

Experience with implementing e-government seamless services has highlighted the impact they can have on agencies' ways of working, structures and culture. The challenge of implementing and operating seamless services has also highlighted the need for change in the internal governance frameworks of public administrations. The following section looks at these impacts to draw out potential lessons; these services can be seen as representing a leading indicator of likely future trends and pressures in e-government more generally.

THE E-GOVERNMENT IMPERATIVE – ISBN 92-64-10117-9 – © OECD 2003

One challenge to effective e-government collaboration is the need for greater accountability. In line with the acceptance of ICT, new public management models have promoted the empowering of managers by freeing up control over inputs and making managers accountable for specified outputs. The consequence is that managers need to have the power of decision over ICT use in their organisation if they are to be effective. Top-down control of ICT, for example by controlling inputs, may reinforce the flight from responsibility for ICT use and related unit outputs by managers who are adverse to ICT.

Seamless online services: progress to date

At the level of information provision, online government portals are well established as a means of gathering together material from different parts of government. Significant co-operation among agencies has been required to enable these portals, but e-government central co-ordinators have also played a key role.

But the development of portals to provide customer-focused information, while challenging, has generally not required addressing differences in agencies' ways of working or technical interoperability issues beyond a certain level. In practice, portals have also been established in some isolation from other service delivery channels (although in a number of countries call-centre and front-counter staff use the co-ordinated online information as a core resource).

The situation changes, however, when integrated transactional services are desired, and these are an important goal in most member countries' e-government strategies. By their nature, such arrangements will require a greater level of collaboration to operate effectively. While many countries are active in this area, the current number of integrated transaction services involving services from more than one agency is small.

Increased collaboration is also needed in order to increase efficiency through shared projects. Shared infrastructure, for example for authentication of key customer groups, can facilitate individual agency initiatives that would otherwise lack a business case. It can also free agencies to focus on their specific content issues. Shared infrastructure is developed centrally, or by a lead agency, to facilitate seamless online services and improve the business case for specific agency initiatives. The use of such infrastructure by agencies can be mandatory or available to be adopted if the infrastructure meets agency needs. For some initiatives, such as whole-of-government portals or secure networks, their value lies in their inclusive nature.

Various middleware solutions are emerging as the dominant approach to technical integration in a number of member countries, allowing information

> ### Box 45. Japan: Shared infrastructure – Kasumigaseki WAN
>
> The Kasumigaseki WAN, which connects all national government head offices, has been in operation since 1997, as a secure intranet for national government. In 2002, it was connected to the Local Government Integrated Administrative Network to link central and local governments. In a first stage, it connects the central government and some 60 local governments (prefectures, major cities), and it is expected to cover all local government by 2003. This joining up is expected not only to improve the level of government services to citizens but also to promote streamlined and efficient administration in central and local governments.
>
> Source: OECD E-Government Working Group.

to flow between the integrated customer interface and the various agency back-office environments. Implementing this approach varies, with different degrees of centralisation involved. The United Kingdom Gateway project aims to provide a common authentication and message hub for use generally across governments, as does Ireland's Reach Agency (see box, below). In Australia, middleware development has advanced primarily in the area of business services and taxation, while arrangements in that sector in Finland use private firms as data collectors and distributors.

> ### Box 46. Mexico: Shared infrastructure and seamless online services – middleware approaches
>
> During 2002, the Government of Mexico launched two experimental projects to build online services under a shared technological platform. Market-based web-services standards were adopted and a total of 20 services from 16 agencies were successfully developed and deployed on top of two alternative platforms for gateway services. The major objective of the project was to demonstrate the interoperability between technological platforms and the ease with which common services could be built using a shared infrastructure.
>
> Source: OECD E-Government Working Group.

On the basis of experience to date, it is evident that the use of agreed standards and approaches and overall levels of co-operation between agencies is more important when agencies share users of their services. Close co-operation is a prerequisite for seamless transaction services, with pooling

> ## Box 47.   **Ireland: Public Services Broker – an approach to seamless services**
>
> In 2000, Ireland adopted the Public Service Broker model to deliver online public services. The Reach Agency (set up in 1999) was mandated to deliver it. Ireland is committed to having all key public services capable of electronic delivery available online, through a single contact point, by 2005. Delivery of public services progress through the framework of the Public Services Broker, which will provide "all day, every day" public services. The Broker's key features are:
>
> - Integration: Providing integrated access to services of central and local government through a single contact point.
>
> - Multiple access channels: Making services available through multiple access channels, including online self-service, and intermediate services through both telephone contact centres and one-stop shops.
>
> - Data security: Providing protected data vaults for secure storage of the personal or business information necessary to facilitate access to public services, while making available to public service agencies only the information that is strictly necessary for the delivery of specific individual services.
>
> *Source*: Irish country submission.

of market research on shared customers, common approaches to presentation, data sharing within government and the authentication required. Customer-focused co-operation can thus be seen as a key organisational principle for e-government; the greater the sharing of citizen or business users, the greater should be the level of co-operation among the relevant organisations.

The resulting landscape may have **clusters of agencies with common customers**, with strong levels of co-operation and common activity within clusters within a broad framework of co-operation across government. However, clusters may bring together programs, products and services without joined-up-services. The integration of working teams from different agencies regarding accountability, financing, organisation, etc. remains a challenge.

Implications of seamless online services

Arrangements for reconciling back-office systems with an integrated customer interface may give the impression that collaboration can be achieved primarily at the technical level, and that other operations can be left

---

Box 48. Sweden: Wilma – information system for processing migration cases

Wilma, the Web-based Information System Linking Migration Authorities, is a new IT support tool shared by Swedish authorities involved in processing migration cases. These authorities are the Migration Board, diplomatic missions (embassies and consulates general), the police border units and the Aliens Appeals Board. The purpose of Wilma is to process information concerning individuals, cases, documents and decisions. IT support allows it to embrace the entire chain, from application for a visa or residence permit at the diplomatic mission to a decision in the case and any appeal. IT support will also promote more efficient monitoring of entries and exits.

The development of Wilma is part of the broad changes aimed at rationalising the multi-authority process affecting the work of diplomatic missions. The improvement involves a basic strategy for applying a holistic approach to developing process-oriented methods. In addition to IT support, the new measures include the development of various forms of collaboration, skills development, strengthening of resources in the form of migration officers posted overseas, a central help desk, improved information, improved follow-up, etc.

Source: Statskontoret.

---

undisturbed. In practice this is unlikely to be the case. In effect, collaborating for seamless e-government services will lead to a deeper engagement between the agencies involved:

● Implementation of **integration models** for online services will require a high level of co-operation for architectures, service delivery policies and standards, implementation methods and schedules, and the co-ordinated acquisition of ICT services and equipment by individual agencies. This will have implications for budgets, business plans, skills and resource management generally. Joint teams may be established to implement new arrangements and may be retained to carry out or co-ordinate maintenance and upgrading.

● Seamless online service **content** will require deeper collaboration on issues such as service quality, presentation of material, decision making on individual cases, dealing with problems, complaints and appeals. This will have an impact on ways of working, decentralised authority and other dimensions of organisational change. Overall **service delivery policies** involving all delivery channels will need to be agreed and co-ordinated by agencies dealing with the specific customer group. There is little point or value in providing a seamless government online service while leaving other channels uncoordinated. In practice, such an approach would be difficult to sustain.

THE E-GOVERNMENT IMPERATIVE – ISBN 92-64-10117-9 – © OECD 2003

- Seamless service delivery will reinforce pressures for **co-ordinated policies** covering the particular customer group. This implies a further layer of collaboration between agencies, building on what may already exist.

Seamless online government service initiatives challenge traditional **accountability** arrangements. Ministers and senior executives are generally responsible for administration of specific legislative or executive instruments. Accountability rules and practices have been developed to clarify responsibility in situations where the service is outsourced, with public administrations and ministers accepting responsibility for the action of non-government providers. The situation may be more complex when the situation involves an agency outside a minister's area of responsibility that provides a service for which the minister is responsible or where cross-agency teams operate. Arrangements need to be made to assign responsibility in these cases. As already occurs in a range of policy areas, responsibilities will invariably be shared. This is not necessarily a problem, so long as there is clarity about the sharing.

Similar comments relate to the issue of **parliamentary or audit scrutiny**. There is a need to preserve the integrity of established overview arrangements while allowing more complex cross-agency activity in the name of more effective and efficient service. Achieving such a balance is difficult, and will require collaboration between service agency and audit and parliamentary officials and representatives to reach an agreed position on information and other requirements.

However, while communication and other change management strategies can be used to align ways of working and culture with the requirements of the overall system, if teamwork and integration are not apparent at senior management levels, performance will not be maximised. There is a danger that the overall objective of the seamless service can become no one's responsibility, and that each agency will aim to maximise its own outputs irrespective of the overall results, and that a cultural divide will persist and detract from the overall performance of teams.

The role of managers and e-government co-ordinators

The **management** of seamless online service initiatives raises its own challenges for agency managers, who are faced with issues of managerial autonomy and collaboration in the context of practical implementation. Member countries' experience suggests that managers and central e-government co-ordinators can facilitate the development of seamless online services with common customers by:

- Developing a **shared vision** for services for the customer group. Political leaders, staff, unions and agency management should endorse the need to collaborate and accept the value of a customer rather than an agency outlook must occur. This includes the development of plans that could usefully cover projected services, implementation paths, agreed standards and procedures and co-ordinated change management strategies

- Increasing use of **formal co-operative mechanisms** such as quasi-contracts or other statements of co-operation spelling out joint responsibilities, objectives, agreed contribution of resources and other aspects of the linked but separate roles of each agency involved. This could involve the adoption of a shared responsibility approach, with a formal agreement covering resource issues and performance of the system. It could also be helpful to create other **incentives for collaboration**, such as a central facilitation fund to focus on design, innovation and incentive structures to facilitate progress.

- Facilitating the development of **customer-focused clusters** to help identify opportunities for closer technical, service delivery and policy integration. Sharing of infrastructure and development or use of a lead agency model will be important for collaboration and would be facilitated by co-ordinated acquisition of ICT within each cluster. Cross-agency teams can help implement and manage specific projects or act as a within-government application service provider to the relevant agencies.

- Taking action to address constraints arising from **internal governance frameworks** in the public administration and adopting team-based

---

Box 49. **Korea: Privacy and data sharing between agencies**

Through e-governmen services, many agencies share administrative information. Documents are issued in electronic format and circulated on the network. The Korean government takes a strong interest in the level of security protection afforded to private information. As a way to ensure security, the network for the shared use of information between administrative agencies is closed and only links government agencies, thus blocking intrusion and hacking.

Strong regulatory measures also exist in the form of various laws (laws on protection of public agency private information) that prohibit access for inappropriate purposes such as disclosure of private information by internal government employees, unauthorised use of personal information and use by unauthorised personnel.

The use of administrative information from another agency is subject to approval by the agency providing the information through a separate approval procedure, after which user registration is required. The perusal of information is possible only after logging in with an administrative electronic signature issued by each administrative electronic signature registration agency.

Source: OECD E-Government Working Group.

---

approaches involving staff from more than one agency. This will require human resource management frameworks, legal frameworks and privacy and data protection.

In practice, collaborative models will involve elements of all of the above approaches, and the approaches will change as co-operation becomes more ingrained.

Skills

OECD countries recognise that ICT-related skills are important not just for ICT production and service industries, but for the economy as a whole. ICT skills have become a new general skill, like literacy or numeracy, and governments have implemented a range of policies to promote the acquisition of basic and advanced ICT skills across the economy. E-government initiatives **increase the importance of the ICT–related skills** required by public administration workforces.

The skills required for e-government are **not simply technical**, as general managers need broad skills to engage in e-government decision making. Necessary skills include basic technical understanding (IT literacy) but also an understanding of information management and the information society. Managers must be able to lead (and not be led by) the organisation's IT department and outside partners, and they must be able to integrate the organisation's ICT strategy with the broader goals of the organisation.

Furthermore, traditional management skills need to be updated and strengthened to deal with the impacts of e-government. Additional competencies are needed in areas such as organisational change, co-operation and collaboration across departments, public-private partnerships, accountability frameworks and performance management.

Four specific **sets of skills** can be identified as essential to successful e-government strategies: information technology (IT) skills, information management (IM) skills, information society (IS) skills, and updated management skills. While the borders of these skill sets are blurred, they provide a useful framework for analysis.

Governments should take steps to identify and ensure the skills needed for effective e-government. This section identifies the types of skills needed for effective e-government, with an emphasis on the skills needed by managers. It also discusses approaches to skill development and training and gives examples of the development and evaluation of e-government skills in various OECD countries.

Who needs e-government skills?

In the early phases of online services, when the Internet was relatively unfamiliar, many projects were driven by IT specialists. General managers lacked interest and/or the required skills. A major challenge is to overcome the view, still held by many employees and managers, that e-government skills are technical matters best left to specialists.

Table 2 gives a broad overview of the types of skills needed by managers and specialists. While general employees and IT specialists need updates and training in new skill areas, managers require the greatest number of new skills.

Table 2.   **Summary of skills needed for e-government**

Skills	Needed by
Information technology	
Basic IT literacy	
Specialist IT skills	All employees, managers and IT specialists
Information managment	
Internal information management	
External information management	Managers and IM specialists
Privacy protection	
Feedback mechanisms	
Information Society	
Understand capabilities of ICT	
Ability to evaluate trends	Managers
Foresee ICT's impact on organisational culture	
Ability to set ICT strategy	
Management/Business	
Organisational change	
Risk management	
Accountability frameworks	Managers
Financing arrangements	
Co-operation and collaboration	
Publict-private partnerships	

Source: OECD.

Skills for all employees. As ICT is increasingly integrated into public administrations, a basic knowledge of technology and the Internet is becoming essential for all employees. Basic IT skills include a working knowledge of applications and how they can improve work quality and efficiency. For employees who do not have these skills, training should be available.

Skills for managers. The adoption of e-government solutions has been hampered by business unit managers' lack of knowledge about how technology can be used as a tool to accomplish or improve government processes. Managers need to be able to work with their organisation's information technology and information management experts to **match government processes with appropriate technical solutions**.

Like all employees, managers need basic IT skills to use ICT effectively. But managers also need to be able to understand the possibilities of ICT, to set or manage the information strategy for the organisation and to deal with the impact of e-government on the organisation. They need to understand how new technology works, how it can be incorporated into existing government functions, and how e-government applications can build new government services and products or open new channels of communication. A solid understanding of the options and their strengths and weaknesses will give managers confidence to negotiate and to specify characteristics for **developing projects that will work**.

Box 50. **Italy: Skills for managers**

After having provided training schemes and resources for e-literacy training for employees, the Department of Public Administration in co-operation with the Department for Innovation Technologies, has recently promoted two new training programmes for managers.

The first one aims at providing top managers (state government) with training to develop information management and information society skills. The programme is run by the National School for Public Administration.

The second one aims at providing top and middle managers of regional and local administrations with training to develop management skills, necessary to meet new organisational needs relating to e-government in the wider context of modernisation plans. This training scheme is part of a broader programme to foster innovation and modernisation in public administrations.

Source: OECD E-Government Working Group.

Given the requirements of e-government, understanding the uses of technology has become a necessary management competency similar to budgeting, strategic planning and personnel management. In addition to basic IT skills, managers also need information management skills, information society skills and updated management skills (see below).

Types of e-government skills

Information technology skills. IT skills are the **technical skills necessary to implement e-government**. They include basic IT literacy (for all employees), and technical skills to design and implement the technical elements (hardware, communication and software) of an e-government initiative (for IT specialists).

Box 51. **Specialist information technology skills**

Strategy and planning

- Develop the organisation's ICT architecture.
- Audit existing technological instruments and their adequacy to the strategy of the organisation.
- Explore software solutions in order to achieve interoperability of data and information.

System development

- Establish the communications network for data, voice, text, image, etc.
- Design the database structure and plan its maintenance.
- Design (or acquire and adapt) software adequate to meet service needs.
- Define requirements for the acquisition of hardware, software, operational and maintenance services.
- Test online services such as Websites, digital TV, electronic kiosks and digital signatures.
- Design instruments for integrating processes and exchanging data.
- Facilitate communication among IT managers, employees and customers.
- Design the system of response to technical problems.

System implementation and maintenance

- Install, integrate and maintain new hardware and software.
- Administer the organisation's network and maintain database structures.
- Implement the system's security measures.
- Implement the organisation's e-payment policy.
- Implement Websites and other output media.
- Evaluate the system continuously through selected performance indicators.

Service and user support

- Receive problems reported by the users and provide technical fixes.
- Design tools for ongoing user training for IT literacy.

Source: Parrado-Díez (2002).
Original source: "Skills Framework for the Information Age": *www.e-skills.com/cgi-bin/cms.pl/120*; UK Cabinet Office (2000), "E-business Skills Assessment Toolkit": *www.e-envoy.gov.uk/publications/guidelines/skills/skills.htm* and document in: *www.e-envoy.gov.uk/publications/rtfs/skills-toolkit-partl.rtf.* Pages visited on 20 July 2002.

While employees and managers increasingly need basic IT skills, most managers and employees do not need specialist skills. Specialist IT skills are for technical staff working in fields such as information technology supplies and services, telecommunications, IT consultancy, multimedia and Internet-based products and services.

THE E-GOVERNMENT IMPERATIVE – ISBN 92-64-10117-9 – © OECD 2003

Information management skills. IM skills cover the **deployment of knowledge resources** within an administration and the sharing of knowledge with partners and others outside the organisation. These skills play an important role in co-ordination and collaboration within the organisation, in creating an organisation that is transparent to the public, and in improving services to citizens and businesses.

Box 52. **Information management (IM) skills for managers and specialists**

Strategy and planning (for managers)

- Understand the organisation's needs in order to design the information system.
- Design the strategy for information management within the organisation and externally.
- Design training programmes for employees and end users.

System development (for IM specialists)

- Identify relevant sources of information for the organisation.
- Design the system of retrieving and keeping information electronically for future use.
- Help to establish the content to be provided for output media and target groups.
- Design the technical system to update and maintain information in different output media.
- Achieve the goals of interoperability of data and information.

System implementation and maintenance (IM specialists)

- Administer and maintain the archive system composed of traditional and electronic means.
- Maintain and update information (knowledge content) from external and internal sources.
- Implement content management system for various output media and target groups.
- Filter and codify information.
- Continuously evaluate the system through selected performance indicators.

Service and user support (for IM specialists)

- Respond to problems with information reported by users.
- Develop and maintain training programmes for employees and end users.

Source: Parrado-Díez (2002).

Box 53. **Information society skills for managers**

Relationship management

- Determine the level of citizen involvement in decision making; set the level of responsiveness.
- Establish long-lasting relationships with ICT suppliers and specialists.
- Define the level of ICT integration with suppliers and other stakeholders.
- Consult staff regarding their needs for e-government services.
- Ensure that staff have adequate support and training.
- Identify common sources of co-operation with partners to achieve seamless government.
- Help to establish governance principles of transparency, responsiveness, responsibility and equity among different partners.

ICT awareness to support organisational strategy

- Understand technology developments related to the organisation's e-government strategy.
- Scan technological tools that can support the organisational strategy.
- Understand the organisation's ICT architecture and the possibilities for innovation and expansion.
- Monitor and understand the activities of suppliers.
- Understand standards for security, privacy and authentication, so that they can be met.
- Understand the principles of risk management.

Implementation management

- Establish the relationships and responsibilities between the supply side (technology) and the demand side (online services).
- Ensure that the end users receive online services in an appropriate manner by meeting quality standards.
- Combine traditional channels and electronic channels of e-government service delivery.

Evaluation management

- Apply project management evaluation to the development of the information system, to the introduction of ICT-related services and to business process re-engineering.
- Identify and apply a library of indicators (with other stakeholders if necessary) in order to evaluate the impact of a strategy of online services adequately.

Source: Parrado-Díez (2002).

IM managers and specialists collectively share responsibility for meeting government's information management needs. IM professionals in government include librarians, archivists, specialists in access to information and privacy, communications managers and record managers; traditional IM skills now need to be updated for ICT use. Additionally, managers need IM skills to set the organisation's strategy for information sharing, privacy protection, transparency and customer feedback mechanisms.

Information society skills. IS skills relate to the ability to use ICT resources to **implement an e-government strategy coherent with the organisation's overall strategy**. They involve understanding the possibilities and the limits of new technology as well as the organisation's overall service strategy, so that the manager can engage in e-government decision making.

IS skills are essential for e-government managers, and comprise areas such as relationship management, ICT awareness to support organisational strategy, e-government implementation management and evaluation management.

Updated management skills. E-government clearly has a major impact on the structure and organisation of public administrations. This impact is so significant that managers must update their traditional managerial skills to meet new organisational needs. Managers need the skills to manage organisational change, improve customer responsiveness, develop accountability frameworks, create incentives for co-operation and collaboration, and manage relationships with the private sector.

E-government skill assessment

The availability of e-government skills in the workforce (and especially among managers) will greatly affect an organisation's ability to adopt an e-government strategy. Finding personnel with the skills needed for an e-government strategy is a problem. Specific skill needs vary by agency and position, and assessment procedures must be simple enough to be practical.

As various examples demonstrate, OECD countries are taking steps to identify and provide the skills and competencies needed for public administrations to efficiently implement e-government initiatives and to maximise their benefits.

Skills development and training

The scale, complexity and rate of change associated with e-government require structured initiatives to ensure that skills remain relevant. The public sector has a range of options for e-government skills development, including hiring of skilled professionals, in-house training and partnering with outside organisations for skills development.

Box 54. **United Kingdom: E-Envoy – an information skills map**

The Office of the E-Envoy in the United Kingdom has outlined a skills map as part of the UK Online Strategy to prepare UK government agencies for e-government adoption. The E-Envoy has defined seven areas for skill development: leadership, project management, acquisition, information professionalism, IT professionalism, IT-based service design and end-user skills.

The E-Envoy has produced a skills assessment toolkit to determine the e-readiness of each agency. The toolkit has been used for departments' self-assessment to gain an understanding of the skills required for planning, implementing and delivering e-government services. The assessment identifies the skills available internally through in-house technology and information professionals and identifies skill gaps that may need to be addressed by expanding staff or outsourcing.

Source: Settles (2002).
Original Source: Office of the E-Envoy (2000), "E-Government: A Strategic Framework for Public Services in the Information Age". Pages visited on 29 June 2002: *www.e-envoy.gov.uk/*

Box 55. **United States: The State of Washington's applications template**

The State of Washington uses the Applications Template and Outfitting Model (ATOM) to bring together policies, infrastructure components and technology and integrate them into a task list. The model also identifies the skill gaps that may need to be filled through training, recruitment or outsourcing. The model defines the following steps:

Step 1: Project definition.

Step 2: Requirements analysis.

Step 3: Detailed design.

Step 4: Project review.

Step 5: Deployment.

Step 6: Systems maintenance.

Source: Settles (2002).
Original Source: Washington State Department of Information Services (2001), "Applications Template and Outfitting Model": Pages visited on 18 August 2002: *www.wa.gov/dis/atom*

Government recruitment of IT and IM specialists should be considered in the context of overall demand, as peaks and troughs in ICT activity affect the availability of skilled staff. Governments generally lag behind the market in remuneration, and thus find recruitment of specialist skills a problem. More flexible arrangements, such as supplementary payments for specific skills, short-term appointments and the use of contractors and private outsourcing organisations are all used to access specialist skills. However, it is important to maintain a core level of expertise within the organisation.

Governments can make better use of the existing workforce (through retention and training), provide more information on skill needs and opportunities (including new pathways to IT jobs) and develop adequate training programmes for various categories of workers (including unemployed and older workers).

Current skills development. OECD countries are taking a variety of approaches to developing and retraining skills. While specific skill sets vary, most countries recognise that technical IT skills are not enough.

Many countries have created Chief Information Officer (CIO) positions both within government organisations and for the whole of government in order to improve organisation practices for the management of information technology and to improve co-ordination and co-operation within government. For example, the United States provides specific training opportunities for CIO positions (see box below).

Box 56. United States: Chief Information Officer (CIO) University

The Chief Information Officer (CIO) University in the United States is an example of a government-sponsored training programme. Learning objectives are organised into 12 broad topics, each of which contains a number of necessary competencies. The 12 topics of the CIO University cover:

1. Policy and organisational.
2. Leadership/managerial.
3. Process/change management.
4. Information resources strategy and planning.
5. Performance assessment.
6. Project/programme management.
7. Capital planning and investment assessment.
8. Acquisition.
9. E-government/electronic business/electronic commerce.
10. IT security/information assurance.
11. Technical.
12. Desktop technology tools.

Source: Settles (2002).
Original source: CIO Learning Objectives (2001), Page visited 11 July 2002: *www.gsa.gov/attachments/ GSA_PUBLICATIONS/extpub/lo-matrix-2001.doc*

Meeting the public's new and changing expectations requires a more agile workforce capable of adapting government processes rapidly in response to changing needs and circumstances. In Canada, the creation of an office for change management demonstrates government's recognition that the success of service transformation depends critically on ensuring that public servants have the knowledge, skills and competencies to deliver public services in an integrated, client-centred, multi-channel environment. However, sustainable change readiness requires leadership and commitment at all levels of the public service.

Box 57. **Canada: Change management skills**

The Organisational Readiness Office's (ORO) approach to building an agile workforce has two main themes: a need for new knowledge and skills to support citizen-centred services; and a need to operate more "horizontally" in partnerships that cut across programmes, departments and even jurisdictions. Workplace cultures are changing, and cultural change of the nature and magnitude expected will not come from the traditional human resources (HR) function alone. The acceptance of individual responsibility for career planning and a focus on adaptability and flexibility also constitute a significant cultural change from the traditional "top-down" approach to skills training and staff development.

The ORO business strategy focuses on identifying alignment between community and organisational interests on HR issues, particularly those related to service transformation. The three key elements of the strategy are awareness and engagement, human-resource capacity building and sharing of management and work practices.

Building on the experience of various initiatives, the IT community is exploring the development of a community-based approach to managing human resources. In the proposed framework, assessment against 15 accepted competency profiles would form the basis of recruitment, staffing, performance management and learning and development plans. The HR framework will include tools, development approaches and procedures that could increase the adaptability and agility of the workforce and increase readiness for change across government. The more profound implication of the framework is that it recognises that there is a place in modern management for input and insights from communities, especially in government workplaces where structural changes to accommodate organisational needs for horizontal integration and collaboration may not be an option.

Source: Canada Country Paper (2002c).

Long-term skills development. Maintaining skill levels is an ongoing process, not a one-time fix. Long-term skills development techniques include providing information to students about possible careers, developing stronger IT skills in secondary schools, assisting in teacher training, making IT careers more attractive (in particular to under-represented groups such as women), ensuring better integration of educational programmes with "real world" problems and helping workers maintain up-to-date skills.

As current IT workers retire, the need for skilled workers is increasing in certain OECD countries. In most countries this is a long-term issue that will require significant change on the part of administrations. Creating systems that unify and simplify citizens' access to information and government services requires new designs, new perspectives and new skills. In an organisation as large and complex as most administrations, such change is necessarily tied to the organisation's history. There must be a concurrent emphasis on retaining a talented workforce with knowledge of the organisation's traditional missions

---

Box 58. United States: Building the e-government workforce

Creating a blended workforce and turning innovative designs into reality present significant challenges, the first of which is recruitment. Overall US government employment has been static or in decline over the last decade. Although there has been some growth in the employment of IT professionals, a significant amount of this growth has come from within existing employee ranks. Recruitment has, in the case of most agencies, been at a maintenance level with turnover in the 2-3% range. There has been little pressure to improve a slow and outdated recruitment and selection system that makes little use of technology.

This stable workforce has become progressively older, with 40% of IT professionals in their 40s and another 29% over age 50. About 50% of the federal IT workforce will be eligible for retirement in the next few years. In an independent study commissioned by the Federal CIO Council, the National Academy for Public Administration stated the challenge as follows:

"It is probably safe to assume that over 50% of the current federal IT professionals, or around 30 000 workers, will retire within the next ten years. Over the same course of time, the federal government is projected to need over 16 000 additional IT workers. This translates to a net need of over 45 000 IT professionals in the next ten years."

Building the e-government workforce in this environment requires change. Change is under way and starts with a human capital plan and a process for developing government IT workers and project managers as well as the skills of the contract workforce that performs much of the government's IT requirements.

Source: United States Country Paper (2002b).

Box 59. **Japan: Timeline of e-government training**

Japan's experience shows that e-government training must be adapted over time to respond to changing requirements.

1960: Implementation of training courses on information systems for national officials. Two courses given for managers and for management analysts.

1968: Decision that "training of key personnel will be implemented uniformly". Automated data processing (ADP) management course created in 1969.

1994: Decision to promote government-wide use of information technology, including steps to enhance human infrastructure and promote IT use. This included securing staff in the information system sector and training core personnel who lead IT services.

1996: Curricula radically revised and courses organised into basic training, specialist technical training and procurement and management training.

1998: Steps to improve the information literacy of employees. New course created for network specialists and Internet-related technology added to the curriculum.

1999: To improve information literacy and increase use of ICTs, courses created for personnel education support training, security specialist training and information analysis and utilisation.

2000: To accompany the updating of local area networks (LANs), the number of courses and terminals increased.

2001: Training courses revised, volume of training courses increased and quality improved in all ministries and agencies (including IT literacy education).

2003: Date scheduled for the introduction of online training.

Source: Japan Country Paper (2002b).

and a strong understanding of how existing systems and strategies can be retooled to support e-government innovations.

Outsourcing to obtain e-government skills

Once skills gaps have been identified, organisations need to decide whether such skills should be provided in house or obtained from external providers. Some basic skills will need to remain in house, for example project management, data security, IT strategy and procurement skills.

Care must be taken in determining which skills to buy in from outside suppliers, taking into consideration risk management, privacy, confidentiality and the security of data, and relationships between business skills and ICT-related skills. This is particularly important for skills which are strategic for an organisation. The following checklist can be used to help determine the need for outsourcing (Parrado-Diez, 2002):

Pre-outsourcing question on skills

- What is the skill level of the organisation for deciding the pre-outsourcing conditions?

IT function and the e-government service

- Is the organisation's IT function clearly defined or definable?
- How critical is the IT service level for the organisation's performance and strategy?
- What are the strengths and weaknesses for internal provision of IT?
- What are the mid- and long-term perspectives for the internal and external provision of IT?

Cost of e-government services and market competition

- Are there hidden costs in outsourcing services?
- What is the total cost of operating e-government services?
- What is the cost of maintaining in house capacity?
- What is the level of competition in the market?

Skills level to manage contracts

- What are the organisation's experience and skill level for managing complex contractual relations?

E-government skill – the role of e-government co-ordinators

While e-government skills needs and arrangements vary considerably among OECD countries, e-government co-ordinators should consider the following points:

- E-government skills are a crucial element of the required mix of skills for managers. It would be of value to **increase awareness of this requirement** at the policy level, backed up by incorporation in management training programmes, criteria for recruitment and assessment of performance.
- Assisting agencies to identify their e-government skills needs through promotion and support for a **standardised assessment approach** would facilitate the task of senior management.
- While requirements can be addressed individually, **agencies have shared training needs**. In conjunction with public-sector training organisations,

e-government co-ordinating units can identify broader skills needs and work with training providers to develop appropriate training packages for different levels of experience and managerial responsibilities.

Public-private partnerships

Engagement with private-sector suppliers has been an integral feature of government use of ICT. Public-private relationships have broadened from the acquisition of products and services such as mainframe computers which governments themselves could not provide, to services such as the operation of computing facilities and direct provision to end users of government services.

Governments' desire to take advantage of the Internet and related technologies has highlighted the role of these relationships. The demand for more sophisticated transactional services adds a level of complexity, with consideration of relatively new technologies such as public key infrastructure. Government organisations faced with these pressures often turn to private providers not just for technical solutions but for the capacity to develop, implement and deliver whole new services.

In addition to providing ICT services *per se*, partnerships are increasingly used as the virtual front counter of government, delivering services to citizens and businesses. This integration of government services with non-government activity can leverage existing infrastructure and existing patterns of citizen and business interaction. While the concept is not new, the integration of online services with related private-sector offerings has highlighted it: integration can add value for both parties. Integration with non-government activity complements seamless government services; from a customer perspective, integration with relevant private-firm or civil-society services may be more relevant than linking government services.

E-government increases the need to engage private partners, for the following reasons:

- As ICT use becomes more widespread, there is a danger that public administrations become too deeply drawn into ICT production issues. Partnerships can free public administrations to allow a **focus on core policy and business issues.**

- Partnerships can be used to access **specialised skills**, for example for software development. Such skills may be difficult or uneconomical to maintain in public administrations or which simply can only be obtained from a private service provider.

- Partnerships can help reduce **risk** by a formal assessment of solutions available in the market and taking a partner that accepts some of the risk

THE E-GOVERNMENT IMPERATIVE – ISBN 92-64-10117-9 – © OECD 2003

Box 60. **Denmark: Innovative partnership arrangements**

There is limited experience with digital projects in public-private partnerships in Denmark. Therefore, both the public and private sectors have been interested in discussing together what is important for forming a successful partnership. Public-private partnerships are often used for complex projects in which knowledge from both the public and private sectors needs to be combined. While the goal must be clear from the start, the solution is most likely to be developed in partnership. This is a challenge and requires both the private and the public organisation to be ready to engage in a close partnership.

The dialogue has led to a joint document, which emphasises three themes:

1. The importance of managerial involvement in setting the project goal, clarifying existing work processes, deciding the space for restructuring and ensuring an overall efficient set-up.

2. The need to improve the efficiency of the public sector. It is important to establish a business case in order to get return on the investment. Furthermore, it is essential to agree on common goals and get the incentives right to achieve them, internally as well as for the partner.

3. To have the necessary flexibility to develop the solution, it is important when calling for tender and writing the contract not always to indicate a specific solution for the project but to concentrate on essential goals and requirements. The use of options can give the flexibility necessary to change that results from an ongoing dialogue.

Source: OECD E-Government Working Group.

associated with the project in return for payment (see section on managing risk and cost).

- Partnerships can help reduce or avoid the need to obtain sufficient **up front funding** to establish a service, by enabling costs to be covered through a series of recurrent payments albeit at a greater cost to government.

- In some cases, partnerships can help **integrate** the delivery of government services into private infrastructure or delivery arrangements to benefit customers and to capture efficiencies.

- Partnerships allow governments to benefit form **economies of scale** for services or processes that are seldom used in any one organisation.

- Partnerships can enable governments to benefit from **innovation** and to capture efficiencies that they otherwise might not be able to.

- Greater experience putting services online within the private sector and civil society can help governments improve their own services.

Governments use partnerships to **learn** from the private sector and civil society, and they can use partnerships to **piggyback** current services already in place.

- Additionally partnerships enable the **private sector to acquire knowledge** of the structure and functioning of the public sector, and thereby improve specific government-oriented solutions.

Types of partnerships

In the broadest sense, the term "public-private partnership" could be used to cover all arrangements where governments contractually engage with a non-government entity to provide goods or services. More narrowly, partnerships involve arrangements whereby work, risk and rewards are shared. In practice, all private supplier relationships are likely to involve elements of partnership, and it is therefore useful to see partnerships as part of a continuum. The partnership management issues they raise need to be addressed as part of the implementation of any e-government project or strategy.

While partnerships differ in complexity and scale, they share many common features:

- They are covered by some form of **contractual arrangement**, specifying outputs, costs, expectations, dispute resolution mechanisms and the like, with the complexity and detail depending on the specific transaction concerned. Whatever the level of flexibility and close working relationships that may be desired, the partnership ultimately needs to operate in a contractual framework.

- Partnerships operate within **established arrangements**, including those of procurement, accountability and reporting. The transparency of such arrangements, particularly involving the privatisation of activities previously undertaken in house has been a major public governance issue for a number of years.

- While governments can use private firms or non-government organisations to supply or deliver goods and services, **responsibility** for the service or programme ultimately rests with government.

Challenges

The more comprehensive and innovative the partnership arrangements, the greater the likely challenge to existing frameworks. The challenges for developing sound partnerships are as follows:

- **Accountability, scrutiny and audit** requirements need to balance providing enough flexibility for innovative arrangements and preserving required levels of oversight of public expenditure. This is a difficult area, although arrangements to achieve this balance are evolving in countries with experience in partnerships both within and outside the ICT area. The use of public-private partnerships should not be at the expense of public scrutiny or compromise accepted privacy or service quality standards. The business case for partnerships should not depend on a lowering of standards.

- The **specification of outputs,** including value for money, can be difficult in arrangements designed to operate over a long period and which allow for future resetting of priorities. If specifications are too tight, it may be necessary to renegotiate – if they are too broad, requirements may be unclear. Arrangements to deal with failure also need to be clear.

- Traditional procurement arrangements aim to transfer risk while retaining control. It needs to be accepted that, in a partnership, both parties should **share the risks** and the benefits. The issue here is management of risk, with the respective risks assigned to the parties best placed to manage them.

- Retaining the public administration's **capacity to manage the relationship** with the private partner is of crucial concern. Managerial awareness and commitment is essential to ensure that the required skills are developed and maintained (see section on skills).

- While structured review and clauses can facilitate review and formal approaches to the market, there is a danger that an existing partnership may be seen as the only approach, thereby effectively **excluding other service providers**.

Ultimately, the overall relationship between the partners is important. The two sides must accept the sharing of risk and rewards, and specify outputs in a way that allows for flexibility. They must accept joint responsibility for project outputs, while acknowledging the differences in accountability and responsibility between government and outside partners. Agencies must balance the need for stability and stable relationships with the need to reassess the value of current partnerships.

Public-private partnerships – the role of e-government co-ordinators

It may be difficult to determine which types of services should be done using public-private partnerships, which should use more conventional supplier relationships and which are best retained within public administrations. For this reason it is important to make available to agencies a **structured approach for assessment**, which allows them to make an appropriate decision. Use of private suppliers can have its costs, in terms of opportunities foregone and transaction costs for establishing and maintaining them.

E-government co-ordinating agencies may wish to develop, in conjunction with procurement authorities and key agencies, an **e-government public-**

private partnerships framework. This would assist in particular the small agencies that often lack sufficient expertise to assess proposals made by potential suppliers of services. Such a framework would also help clarify what is allowed under existing procurement frameworks, and help identify areas where change would be beneficial. It is also important for broader policy frameworks (regarding for example the use of local ICT suppliers) to be flexible enough to enable decisions to be made on the merits of each case.

An examination in each country by e-government co-ordinators and other relevant agencies, including national audit bodies, of audit and accountability arrangements covering private supplier relationships would help clarify requirements and give further guidance to agencies.

Managing risk and cost[4]

Most governments experience problems when implementing large IT projects. Budgets are exceeded, deadlines are overrun and often the quality of the new system is far below the standard agreed when the project was undertaken. Moreover, governments are not alone in failing. Evidence suggests that private sector companies have similar problems. The Standish Group, for example, estimates that only 28% of all IT projects in 2000 in the US, in both government and industry, were successful with regard to budget, functionality and timeliness. 23% were cancelled and the remainder succeeded only partially, failing on at least one of the three counts.

Large public IT projects can pose great political risks. Ministers and governments are held accountable for the failures and the accompanying waste of taxpayer money. These significant economic losses comprise not only outright waste in exceeded budgets and abandoned projects, but also – and equally importantly – lost opportunities for enhanced effectiveness and efficiency. The inability of governments to manage large public IT projects threatens to undermine efforts to implement e-government.

Public management systems

Public sector organisations operate in settings very different from the private sector, and these differences are important for understanding why governments fail and what challenges project managers face. Change is inherent in implementing public policies. Laws are changed, priorities shift, and implementation accordingly has to adjust. However, changing specifications for IT systems that are under construction is likely to make the systems more complicated, blur agreements with providers and bloat budgets. Small policy changes can require major changes in IT structures. Similarly, the time allowed for legislation to come into effect is often much too short for proper IT systems to be built and launched. Unrealistic deadlines set by the highest political authorities need to be addressed.

If failure is to be avoided, implementation must be taken into account when policies are formulated. Furthermore, special standards of accountability and transparency apply to the public sector. This means that failure is often widely publicised and that top-level civil servants and politicians are held accountable for very technical projects over which they may have little influence.

In many countries, rapid policy change, higher standards of accountability and short deadlines are unavoidable governance facts. Nevertheless, it might be possible to raise awareness of the interdependency of policy and implementation issues when it comes to e-government. At the very least, risks inherent in the governance settings should be identified and better managed.

Budgeting for risk

Public sector budgeting systems can encourage the funding of large and highly visible IT projects. Small projects cannot justify new funds and do not command attention during budget negotiations. Furthermore, large, expensive and spectacular projects are often favoured because these projects are more easily communicated as evidence of political action and response to a problem. This is unfortunate, since the risk of failure is proportional to the size of the project. Very large projects, i.e. expensive, long-term and complex initiatives, often fail.

A radical approach, increasingly adopted in the private sector, is to avoid large projects altogether, opting for small projects instead. One expert has called this change a shift from "whales to dolphins". Adopting dolphins does not mean breaking big projects into small modules. Rather, it involves a shift to a different way of working and thinking, with total project timeframes of no more than six months, technical simplicity, modest ambitions for business change, and teamwork driven by business goals.

Although large IT projects should be avoided wherever possible, government is often very big business. Millions of citizens are served, regulated or taxed, and thousands of employees use the systems. Therefore, it is improbable that all IT projects in the public sector can be made smaller. Where big projects are

---

Box 61. New Zealand: Funding for risk

In New Zealand, risk-based funding rules for complex projects have been developed. Using quantitative risk analysis, each risk is assessed along with its impact and probability. Thus, the fiscal impact of a project's risks can be made explicit to decision-makers.

Source: OECD Policy Brief "The Hidden Threat to E-Government" (2001).

---

unavoidable, they should be divided up into self-contained modules that can be adjusted to changes in circumstances, technology and requirements.

Managing new technologies

New technologies are tempting because they often promise better solutions and fascinating possibilities for business change. More often, they promise solutions that enable an organisation to implement IT without changing its business processes. It is therefore not surprising that public sector organisations keep trying to develop systems based on new technologies. Experience shows, however, that systems built on emerging and unknown technologies are very susceptible to failure. In some instances the potential benefits might warrant taking such huge risks; most often this is not the case.

Risk of failure can be reduced by using well-proven approaches or even better, standard software, although this will often imply that business processes have to be adapted to the possibilities offered by the IT system. The application of common commercial practice, rather than custom software, has proven time and again to be the most successful solution. Where the use of unproven technologies is unavoidable, a testing programme for the new technology in question carried out prior to the contract with the supplier could help identify, assess and manage the risks.

Responsibility

There is no such thing as an IT project in isolation. Rather, every IT system should be seen as a tool and means to other ends – notably a change in business processes. IT projects are thus business projects and must be led by top management and not by IT experts.

Clear lines of responsibility and accountability are needed for good project management. It must be clear at the outset *who* will be held

---

Box 62. **United States: Risk and responsibility**

One of the most important reasons for resolving the Y2K problem in the United States was the attention from top-level management. Because the Federal Government designated it as the foremost management objective in 1999, management policies, practices and processes were all refocused and managers were held accountable for coping with Y2K. Dealing with the risk of failure became the mission, even though it was a technological problem.

Source: OECD Policy Brief "The Hidden Threat to E-Government" (2001).

accountable for delivery, *how* performance will be measured and sanctioned and *when* assessment will take place. Thus, in the public sector the role of IT must be reflected in the way organisations are managed. An isolated IT office is sufficient for internal technical applications but not for critical business applications that change the face of the agency and that affect critical legal and business issues.

Involving employees

The potential impact of IT initiatives on employees and their jobs must be recognised. A comprehensive strategy for managing change should be part of project planning. This should include targeted communications, effective and appropriately timed education and training, and user support plans to prepare employees and other stakeholders for change.

Employees who use technology should thus be involved as early as possible in project management and communication. Close consultation with client groups and representatives helps build ownership and commitment. Extensive user participation in systems development and testing is essential.

Risk identification

Risk identification and management are paramount features of successful IT project management. Some countries have well-developed guidelines and practices in this field; others still have something to learn. Independent consultants from outside the administration can help identify risks. The use of such independent reviews at key stages of a project can provide a valuable snapshot of the health of the initiative. However, expert advice only makes sense if project management deals promptly and thoroughly with the issues raised. It is interesting to note, however, that many failures can be explained by poor compliance with otherwise very good guidelines and existing good practice. Knowledge management and management control systems adapted to the national culture must also be put in place.

The general lesson is not that governments should not take any risks; rather, governments must identify risk, determine which risks they are willing to take, and manage the relevant risk within appropriate governance structures. Governments must balance risk management with innovation and value creation. When governments have complex e-government plans, they must ensure that these plans are feasible (see also section on vision statement/plan), and not try to do too much at once. This idea has much in common with the conventional e-commerce wisdom: "Think big, start small, scale fast."

Monitoring and evaluation

It is necessary to monitor and evaluate e-government to understand demand, assess the benefits to users of alternative proposals and evaluate the effectiveness of proposals in meeting their objectives. Evaluation is needed to argue the case for new projects and expenditure, to justify continuing with initiatives, to allocate additional IT funds, to assess progress towards programme goals and to understand impacts. Additionally, monitoring and evaluation can assist with programme consolidation and selection of standards. OECD countries recognise the importance of this issue, and e-government policies and strategies reflect this recognition.

A number of promising initiatives exist in this area, although OECD countries acknowledge the need for improvement. Current efforts may be suitable for evaluating online services but do not take into account the back-office changes that accompany e-government.

The section on online services discusses a four-tier model for evaluation of online services, this section discusses back-office monitoring and evaluation. It gives an overview of current practices and discusses specific tools that have been identified over the course of the project as being of particular importance (assessment of costs, benefits, demand and service quality).

Background and context

Current tools for programme and project evaluation provided by the private sector are a good starting point to evaluate e-government initiatives but should also take into account the public dimension of e-government in order to be effectively applied. Evaluation tools in this context demonstrate the limits to capturing the qualitative and/or fiancial value generated by large ICTs projects. (Van Gils, 2002):

- E-business evaluation tools like the **DMR Results Chain, the E-business Balanced Scorecard** and **Cranfield's Process Model** have been successful in evaluating e-business, but to be suitable for e-government, they would need to incorporate social dimensions and the expected benefits of governance goals.

- The **EFQM Excellence Model** was introduced in 1992 for self-assessment of quality in organisations. Building on this model, the **Common Assessment Framework (CAF)** was designed for self-assessment in the public sector. While both frameworks are useful for government assessment, neither takes into account the difficulty of measuring the benefits of ICTs.

Obstacles to evaluation

Monitoring and evaluation of government programmes is generally difficult, given the frequent lack of clarity of objectives owing to the different and often competing views held by different stakeholders. In addition, overlapping initiatives and policies and continuous fine-tuning of initiatives complicate monitoring and evaluation efforts. The fact that e-government is relatively new and that there are few advanced services means fewer models and actual outcome experiences that can be used for benchmarking.

These problems are magnified when attempting to monitor and evaluate e-government programmes. ICT projects are hard to evaluate because of the pervasive nature of ICTs, the integration of ICT goals with policy goals and the organisational changes that necessarily accompany e-government initiatives. Effective evaluation requires good metrics, regular monitoring and reporting, disciplined and professional use of robust evaluation frameworks and the use of long-term evaluation practices. These qualities depend on a government's overall evaluation culture. Table 3 summarises some of the barriers to e-government evaluation and gives various examples.

Table 3. **Obstacles to evaluating e-government**

Obstacle	Example
Lack of clarity of objectives – stated goals may not have associated measures of progress; there may be multiple objectives	Hard to measure "quality of life"
Hard to define success	If people are spending more time online, is that good or bad?
Easy to be too ambitious	Several countries have set targets of "al services online" by specific dates. But not all services are appropriate to put online
Information paradox	The benefits of ICT investment may not be visible for some time (see OECD Growth Study)
Question of who are the clients; multiple clients	Should one evaluate benefits for the users, the employees, the government at large, partners, etc.?
Hard to measure shared benefits	Shared infrastructure, multiple projects benefiting from shared portal, etc.
Private sector tools may not work for governments	Governments place importance on social values that are not incorporated into private sector tools and objectives
Available indicators may not be the good ones	Current indicators (such as number of employees with Internet connections) are helpful, but have limits
Government definitions and methodologies vary from one country to the next	Collecting data is easier at the local level, but at that level administrations are highly decentralised
Incentives to misstate evaluation results	If an organisation succeeds in saving money, telling others may result in their losing that money
Challenge of sharing results	Hard to get organisations to report unsatisfactory results
What you measure may become focus of organisation	Il you measure number of services online, but not service quality, priority will be on putting services online but not on service quality

Source: OECD.

To overcome these barriers and monitor and evaluate e-government successfully, a number of issues must be addressed:

- **A framework for assessment must be prepared prior to initiation**, as well as a framework for evaluating efficiencies once the project is completed. The process to be improved or replaced by the proposed arrangements must be clearly defined. The project's full costs, including the costs of managing the associated organisational changes, also need to be identified. Furthermore, "success" needs to be clearly defined and if possible linked to the broader goals of the organisation and the national strategy. Both implementers and evaluators must agree on the definition of success.

- The knowledge that the evaluation may be used to determine the survival of the project or future funding creates a danger that the organisation's sole focus will be to meet specific targets. This is particularly a problem when the indicators for e-government evaluation may not be representative of the programme's goals. To the extent possible, **e-government indicators should be designed to reflect programme goals.**

- For an evaluation to be useful, **results need to be available to decision makers at the right time**. When information on longer-term outcomes is not available in the requisite timeframe, alternative indicators should be used. Evaluation procedures should be realistic and focused on specific issues of value. All e-government evaluation will inevitably be a compromise between rigorous evaluation on the one hand and practical realities on the other.

- The **evaluation process should be unbiased and independent**, so that it can be used as a basis for revising e-government initiatives. It should also be non-threatening to participants. It should be general enough to apply to more than one agency, initiative or programme.

- E-government evaluations should be **based on a mixture of qualitative and quantitative indicators**. Qualitative indicators are useful because they may be better suited to some e-government benefits (such as improved quality of life) than quantitative indicators. However, qualitative indicators may be difficult to use when comparing projects and levels of success. Quantitative indicators are useful because they are more readily comparable and can be used to demonstrate concrete benefits. However, quantitative indicators are not always suited to e-government goals, and there is the danger of overvaluing their importance. As evaluation efforts become more advanced, there may be a greater reliance on qualitative measures.

- The evaluation process should take into account both **direct and indirect costs and benefits**. While indicators should be based on stated targets, they should also be flexible enough to take into account unexpected outcomes or be adapted for a later point in time.

THE E-GOVERNMENT IMPERATIVE – ISBN 92-64-10117-9 – © OECD 2003

- Finally, **e-government should be repeatedly evaluated** over time. The process should include pre-analysis, implementation analysis and post analysis.

Benchmarking

Evaluating national policy. Evaluating e-government programmes at the national level involves assembling data from a wide range of inputs, using consistent definitions and methodologies. Benchmarking sectors or national efforts with other sectors and programmes requires common approaches and definitions.

It is much more difficult to measure e-government at the national level than to evaluate specific projects. Evaluation **requires a large degree of compatibility between data from different agencies**, but their data are rarely comparable.

Current efforts to evaluate national policy have largely focused on the evaluation of online services. These studies tend to focus on: online service breadth (*e.g.* the number of services provided); online service span (*e.g.* the customer target group to which online services are delivered); online service depth (*e.g.* the complexity of the online services provided); and to a lesser extent online service quality (*e.g.* the extent to which online services achieve their stated objectives). However, these measures are only for online services, and are not well suited to evaluating e-government at the back-office level (except for advanced services, which generally require back-office changes). Specific measures that can be used for a broader e-government evaluation include:

- Pre-requisites for online services (*e.g.* Internet penetration, necessary skills, etc.).
- Level of shared infrastructure (*e.g.* are different agencies sharing the same infrastructure resources, or is each obliged to build its own?).
- Channel delivery strategy and/or existence of a one-stop shop (*e.g.* one point of access for all government services, whether national, regional or local and whether all agencies are working through it).
- Level of regulatory framework and enforcement at national level (*e.g.* privacy and security standards, authentication).
- Prevalence of national standards.
- Extent of co-operation and co-ordination among organisations.
- Level of public-private partnerships.
- Existence of financing mechanisms supporting e-government.

Box 63. **Italy: E-government observatory**

The Department of Public Administration has established as a pilot project an observatory to examine the impact of ICT on public administration. At both central and local level, the project aims at measuring quality improvements in the provision of a public service (mainly to citizens and businesses, but also to other branches of local and central government) as well as efficiency gains within public administrations. The observatory aims at providing policy makers as well as managers with a tool allowing more thorough decision concerning both e-government policy and projects.

Source: Corsi and Gullo (2002).

International benchmarking. Measuring progress against other countries (international benchmarking) is a common way of determining the success of national policy. International benchmarking can be a powerful tool for capturing the attention of ministers and generating political commitment to achieving certain national goals. However, international benchmarking studies to date lack accuracy and are judgmental, so they can conceal as much as they reveal. Finding common measures across countries is a very difficult task, especially as countries take different approaches to the provision of online services. Finding effective and comparable measures is also more difficult when dealing with complex variables such as quality *versus* the more simple quantity of services online. For this reason, existing statistical surveys tend to focus on the aspects of e-government that are easier to measure, such as percentage of services online or use of e-government services, but do not take into account the more complex and back-office changes that are fundamental to e-government. A summary of existing statistical surveys is given in Annex 2.

Current benchmarking studies are limited for the following reasons:

- They tend to focus on the supply side and do not generally include the demand for and use of e-government.
- They tend to be output rather than outcome oriented.
- They focus on government-to-citizen and government-to-business interactions, but do not measure government-to-government or government-to-employee interactions.
- The process is not transparent to governments and does not include a clear methodological statement.
- The process is not internationally agreed (each survey employs its own definitions and measuring tools, and other countries are not consulted).

Box 64. **Post-implementation reviews for e-government projects**

Post-implementation guidelines provide evaluation requirements to be included by agencies in post implementation reviews (PIR). Once a project has reached its end, a PIR should be conducted, generally 3-12 months later. The focus of the PIR is to provide an assessment of the implemented project, including an evaluation of the development process and indicate the extent to which the organisation's investment decision-making processes are sustaining or improving the success rate of IM/IT projects.

Three essential areas have to be evaluated as part of a complete PIR:

● Citizens/end users: Surveys should be conducted to determine users' satisfaction with the end product. Many of the intangible benefits identified at the outset will relate to how citizens and end users feel about the final projects.

● Mission/programme impact: A close look should be taken to determine whether the system implemented has achieved its intended effect and whether this effect still fits mission goals. There should be a focused look at how well the project supports the organisation's various processes. An assessment should also be made of other project-specific aspects, such as an estimate of the cost savings achieved, compliance with the information technology architecture, along with evaluations of the information product (accuracy, timeliness, adequacy and appropriateness of information) and identification of additional maintenance or security issues.

● Technical capability: Finally, an evaluation should be made of the technical aspects of the project, both current and future. This evaluation may focus on such factors as the competency of the workforce to use the new system, employee satisfaction or retention, the extent to which advanced technology was used and the methodological expertise of the development team.

Source: Van Gils (2002).

Original Source: IM/IT Investment Evaluation Guide, based on *www.cio-dpi.gc.ca/emf-cag/investeval/ieg-gei00_e.asp*

● A country's overall performance is measured on the basis of only a small number of elements.

● No account is taken of countries' priorities, approaches or e-government objectives.

Standard OECD statistics. Using standard statistics to make international comparisons of e-government is not easy. Not only is it difficult to delineate the concept of e-government (it may range from publishing basic government

> ### Box 65. **The Netherlands: The need for evaluation tools**
>
> A recent Dutch study proposes developing a common system of concepts for measurement of e-government and international benchmarking. At present, there is scarcely any quantitative material available, at either the international or national level. The few internationally comparable publications often include no more than a few readiness indicators. While there are valuable national studies, they do not lend themselves to international comparison or benchmarking.
>
> To measure e-government, OECD countries need to develop a measurement tool which covers all relevant aspects and indicators of e-government. Each country would measure and analyse its situation with regard to e-government using the same set of research tools, preferably during the same time period. Some adaptation would be possible, *e.g.* large countries might use a larger sample than smaller ones. In their report to the OECD, countries would be able to contextualise results in the light of specific national characteristics, such as the structure and extent of the government.
>
> As a result, the benchmarking of e-government would be based on primary data and internationally comparable. However, it is also important to take countries' specific context into account when evaluating its implementation of e-government. A benchmarking exercise should offer space for considering qualitative aspects along with the quantitative data, thus providing a more nuanced view of each country's position.
>
> *Source:* Holland (2002).

information on the Internet to letting citizens engage in dialogue with elected officials), but governments have different structures for service delivery and e-government co-ordination.

The statistics produced by OECD countries often refer to evaluation of national policies on the information society, but even here the statistics may vary from country to country. The OECD's *Measuring the Information Economy* (2002b) provides some internationally comparable statistics on aspects of e-government.

Very few countries implement dedicated surveys of e-government, *i.e.* surveys in which government agencies are asked how they use ICTs as tool for improved service and communication. Countries that do use such surveys include Australia, Canada, Denmark and Norway.

The OECD Working Party on Indicators for the Information Society (WPIIS) is currently developing guidelines and model surveys covering aspects of e-government. The model questionnaire on measuring ICT use and e-commerce currently includes one e-government question for enterprises, which asks about business use of the Internet to communicate with public authorities. For households and individuals, the model questionnaire includes questions about obtaining information from government Websites, downloading or submitting forms and other dealings with government.

WPIIS is aiming eventually to create separate modules on e-government in the enterprise and household/individual model questionnaires by further developing the current questions, and adding one new one. By taking on this task, WPIIS hopes to act as a forum for developing common indicators on e-government demand and use. However, no plans exist for developing guidelines and model questionnaires for ICT use in government; the very different structures of government would make it difficult or impossible to compile comparable statistics.

Evaluation of e-government activity

A focused examination on **elements of e-government activity** would be very valuable to most OECD countries. Cost-benefits assessments can assist agency decision makers in facing specific choices when implementing projects or help central e-government co-ordinators identify priorities for limited central funds.

Monitoring and evaluation of e-government is a broad area. The following discussion focuses on aspects judged priorities by the project working group, namely: costs and benefits, demand and service quality.

Cost/benefit analysis. Discussions of the utility of cost-benefit analyses for e-government initiatives are ongoing. Some argue that countries should not rely on cost-benefit analysis as the single basis for public budgeting and that other non-financial gains must be considered. Cost-benefit analysis is typically readily calculable for bricks and mortar projects like dams and roads, but is less obviously of value for government initiatives where the expected benefit may be public convenience or even improved public perceptions of public services (Reeder, 2002).

For example, there is considerable debate regarding the economic value of small time savings. If the public, on average, spends 30 minutes less time waiting in line for a driver's licence to be issued, are those small increments truly recoverable and put to other economically productive uses? Put differently, if 100 000 individuals each save 30 minutes once a year, has the economy realised the equivalent of 25 work years in savings?

Cost and benefits need separate measures before they can be combined into cost/benefit analysis. A few areas for consideration include:

● Available tools to measure the costs of an e-government project and justify launching an initiative.

Box 66. **Australia: National evaluation of e-government, February 2003**

In early 2002, the Australian National Office for the Information Economy (NOIE) commissioned a study into the demand for and benefits of e-government. The aim of the study was twofold: i) the development and application of a methodology to assess the success of the Commonwealth's government online programme through an analysis of past and future demand, benefits and return of investment; and ii) the development of a methodology for measuring the success of future online initiatives allowing comparison. Preliminary findings of the study were released in November 2002.

The findings – Demand

From 1997/98 to 2001/2002, the Prime Minister's commitment and agency client service strategies appear to have provided the major stimulus for agencies to offer services online to citizens and businesses.

The study found that there is ongoing demand for online services and that users believe significant benefits are available. It found that future demand for online government services might increase by approximately 30% in the period 2002 to 2004.

Citizens and businesses indicated that in the next twelve months they would use the Internet to access Commonwealth Government information related to education, health, taxation, employment, weather, community support, and to a lesser extent family assistance information.

Benefits to users

The vast majority of users of government online services see significant benefits from being able to access services online. 86% of government online users felt that the overall benefit of government online was either significant (36%) or moderate (50%). However, only 45% were able to quantify actual cost savings associated with interacting with Government online compared to traditional channels.

As a result of interacting with government online:

- over 80% of all users indicated a moderate to significant improvement in the ease of finding information;
- approximately 75% indicated some or significant improvement in service quality;
- 75% saw either some (24%) or significant improvement (51%) in their ability to make decisions;
- over 80% of businesses and nearly 90% of government employees saw either some or significant improvements in the quality of their decision-making; and
- access to public records was considered more open by 68% of all users.

Box 66. **Australia: National evaluation of e-government, February 2003** (*cont.*)

Benefits to government

The study estimated potential financial benefits over the period 2000 to 2004 to government agencies through a reduction in costs:

- 67% expected to reduce costs significantly due to improved business processes;
- 64% expected to reduce costs significantly by directly reducing costs of servicing – i.e. direct cost reductions, such as advertising, printed material, staff costs and client management costs; and
- 17% expected to reduce costs significantly by using multi agency delivery channels.

Future beneficial features

The study found that citizens and businesses considered that there would be further benefits from features, such as:

- a seamless online government presence that provides more information, structured so that it is easy to find and does not require an understanding of how the government works; and
- further integration and clustering of services across agencies at all levels of government.

The final results from the study are available on the NOIE website.

Source: www.noie.gov.au

- Comparing costs of an e-service and the traditional equivalent.
- Investment and uptake costs.
- Operational costs, including maintenance and training.
- Long-term costs, including the cost of updating systems and depreciation.
- Expected cost savings in the longer term.
- Opportunity costs of launching an e-government initiative.

The benefits flowing from ICT investments can be difficult to identify, given the integration of ICTs into broader policy goals and organisational change. More specifically, assessing the benefits of e-government initiatives to governments and to service users is difficult because:

- Benefits may be unclear, overlapping and reliant on the performance of other initiatives.
- Goals may be expressed in terms of putting services online, or putting infrastructure in place. While these goals can be evaluated in their own

Box 67. **Australia: The Victoria Government Online intermediate benefits review, 2001**

The Victorian State government, a leader of e-government efforts in Australia, undertook an intermediate benefits review (IBR) of its government online programme. The goal was to provide an accurate summary of delivered and planned GOL benefits and funding in Victoria. An independent consultant conducted the IBR in three phases over a 20-week period commencing 13 November 2000. Some 460 online government projects encompassing 155 programmes, 56 agencies and a sample of 274 citizens, as well as in-depth analysis of 26 individual case studies, were surveyed. At the time of the IBR, 46% of programmes were described as complete and 54% were still in progress.

Phase 1 involved surveying project data from agencies of the Victorian Public Service over a four-week period. As it was assumed that benefit tracking was not a core competency of all Victorian government agencies, the consultant hosted pre-survey briefing sessions to prepare the respondents for calculating expected benefits and cost savings. Agencies were asked to specify expected and delivered benefits of social worth ranging from nil to significant and agency worth in financial terms across a range of bands. Finally, the agencies were asked to estimate the extent to which benefits had been realised and what risks might prevent the benefits from being realised. Agencies were asked to supply where possible or at least identify suitable metrics and baseline data for future time series analysis. When the survey ended, the consultant performed a quality-control analysis of the data before freezing the database.

Phase 2 involved surveying a sample of users of GOL services (Victorian citizens, businesses and departments) to confirm the benefits identified in phase 1 from a social perspective and identify unexpected benefits and gaps where benefits were not achieved.

Phase 3 concerned future funding recommendations.

The benefits framework was built on the basis of GOL objectives, benefits estimations developed by the consultant and validation of data by opinion surveys of the population.

Source: Van Gils (2002)
Original source: Victoria Government Online – Intermediate Benefits Review, 2001 – www/egov.vic.gov.au/Victoria/StrategiesPoliciesandReports/Reports/intermediateBenefitsReview/ibr.htm

terms, they do not take into account uptake or the actual benefits desired or achieved by end users.

● It may not be clear who actually benefits from e-government initiatives (government, users, employees, etc.), especially as some of the beneficiaries

144

may be unintended. It is also unclear whose benefits should be counted when adding up benefits.

- Benefits from shared arrangements such as common infrastructure can be difficult to assess.
- Benefits include both direct outputs (such as the reduction in the time needed for compliance by small businesses using online services) and broader outcomes (such as the impact of the reduced time on business viability).
- Benefits will inevitably involve elements that are both quantifiable (*e.g.* cost and time savings) and non-quantifiable (*e.g.* improved service quality), raising the issue of valuation of non-financial benefits.
- Benefits will not be static, but will change over the life of the initiative as user expectations evolve.

In practice, the evaluation of benefits has focused on estimates of efficiencies in government and improved convenience for users. These estimates are often made at the project initiation stage, to justify commencing a project. Assessment of realised benefits resulting from initiatives also needs to be emphasised to identify lessons learned from project implementation and operation.

Assessing demand. A major focus of e-government activity has been increasing the supply of online services with relevant targets. Given their relative novelty, many services were developed without reference to potential demand. However, as services become more complex and include transactional services, **assessment of demand becomes critical** to ensure that the benefits of initiatives both to governments and to end users match the costs involved.

As for other forms of service delivery, measuring demand for potential online services is complex. Issues to be addressed include identifying the potential pool of users, assessment of accessibility, including general online access by the target group, ease of use and the requirements of groups with special needs, such as the disabled.

Experience has shown the difficulty of predicting usage patterns before the online services are implemented. Potential users cannot be expected to have identified specific requirements for online services, as these emerge only in the light of actual experience. As services become more complex, the need for pilot testing and prototyping becomes more important. As services are implemented, **structured feedback arrangements** enable adjustments to be made in the light of experience.

Box 68. **Finland: E-government-related surveys**

Since 1999, the Ministry of the Interior has made annual surveys of citizens' views on the delivery of electronic services by the public administration. The results have suggested that while citizens are familiar with services provided by their own municipality or local state authority, they have little awareness of other public-sector electronic services. These limited surveys indicate that Finns support the development of public e-service, but they do not reveal much about the level of citizen demand for e-government.

As a part of building the national citizen portal, the Ministry of Finance carried out a user survey of 100 citizens and civil servants in 2000. The results showed that citizens recognised the need for a portal that could provide: i) information about public-sector organisations and their services; ii) advanced electronic services for which transactions are possible; and iii) feedback mechanisms on specific questions.

For regional portals, the most commonly used services were public services. Even though the attitude towards these services was positive and they were frequently used, these services were also seen as the ones that needed the most development.

The Chamber of Commerce and the Association of small and medium-sized enterprises have also conducted several surveys on companies' interest in electronic services.

Source: OECD report on E-Government in Finland (2003).

Service quality. Measuring service quality is of particular importance for e-government, as most governments regard improvement of the quality of public services as an important objective of e-government programmes. Quality standards, which will vary for individual projects, need to be developed in the context of broader service charters and standards. The quality of e-government services is often assessed as citizen satisfaction, measured through interviews or online questionnaires. Frequent **surveys of citizen satisfaction** are of particular importance in e-government, as customer's expectations and habits are evolving rapidly in a changing service environment. Results from these surveys may be used to identify improvements that meet user needs by making services more accessible and effective. Results may also be used to update service quality standards.

Monitoring and evaluation – the role of e-government co-ordinators

Improving monitoring and evaluation is a major task for e-government co-ordinators. Improvements in this area will require a balance between the practical needs of agencies – producing information that will actually be

Box 69.   **United Kingdom: The People's Panel**

In 1998, the Cabinet Office's Modernising Public Services Group set up the "People's Panel" to be better able to provide the services that people want. Citizens' panels had already been used in local government for many years, but this initiative was a world first at the national level. The panel is composed of 5 000 members and is representative of the UK population in terms of age, gender, region and a wide range of other demographic indicators. An additional 830 members were recruited from ethnic minorities to ensure that the sample of minority groups is large enough to be used for quantitative research.

The government is using the People's Panel for many service delivery issues on a regular basis and has recommended that departments use it when starting and implementing e-government projects and programmes.

For instance, in April and May 2000, the Cabinet Office's Performance and Innovation Unit (PIU) created six focus groups from the People's Panel to get a better understanding of people's attitudes towards electronic delivery of public services. The findings have been used by PIU in compiling their report on e-government, "Electronic Government Services for the 21 Century".

Source: People Panel's homepage: *www.cabinet-office.gov.uk/servicefirst/index/pphome.htm*

Box 70.   **Australia: Victoria Tourism Online**

Victoria Tourism Online has performed customer surveys to establish performance baselines, conducted focus groups with representative users and participated in industry forums to understand the likely need for tourism services online. This knowledge of customer demand is cited as a critical element of the project's success.

Source: Detailed Benefits Report, Multimedia Victoria Government Online, Intermediate Benefits Review, Phase 2, 27 June 2001.

used – and the difficulty of maintaining a quality evaluation and analysis process. While countries' priorities will differ, the need to better articulate the benefits of e-government activity means that the focus should be on the benefits of initiatives. Without clearly stated benefits, e-government implementers cannot expect political and public support. E-government co-ordinators should consider the following action:

● Establishing a network of practice across key agencies, focused on e-government evaluation issues.

> ### Box 71. United Kingdom: Customer segmentation and website testing
>
> The Office for National Statistics (ONS) has used a number of means to better understand customers' needs. Throughout 2001, customer-segmented focus groups examined its product portfolios, the type of data provided and how best to deliver it – on paper or electronically via the Website, for example. Customers were segmented by type and by how frequently they used the data. On the basis of this research, the ONS decided how to deliver data and services for each group.
>
> The ONS launched a new Website in 2001 after conducting the focus groups and laboratory usability testing to understand how its users navigated to find the information they needed.
>
> These findings were systematically used as part of a development programme. Users are being involved at key stages of development and will influence the look, feel and functionality of the site.
>
> *Source:* National Audit Office (2002).

> ### Box 72. Canada: Service quality and Common Measurement Tool (CMT)
>
> The CMT was developed by the Canadian Centre for Management Development's Citizen-Centred Service Network to improve the measurement of client satisfaction. The CMT asks questions about service delivery at the operational level. It is conceived around five key elements: client expectations, perceptions of the service experience, satisfaction levels of importance, and priorities for improvements. There is a core set of questions for inter-jurisdictional comparisons of client satisfaction in a few key areas of service delivery, as well as a larger question bank from which organisations can choose based on their needs and particular situations.
>
> *Source:* www.cio-dpi.gc.ca/si-as/tools-outils/tools-outilstb_e.asp

- With the use of this network, developing a framework for assessment of demand, benefits and user satisfaction for use by agencies to assess individual agency projects.

- Gaining agreement of central budget authorities to use this framework as a standard, acceptable method for assessing these impacts for the purpose of budget decision making.

4.4. What could go wrong?

Identifying the potential gains from e-government is one thing; actually realising them is another. Implementing ICT projects, especially large-scale projects that can have a major impact on service quality improvements or efficiencies, raises a number of problems, many of which relate particularly to operating within government. Some of these problems are listed below; following the approaches outlined in this report will assist in reducing these risks.

- As with projects outside government, **projects must be managed effectively**. The section on managing risk and cost, as well as the OECD publication "The Hidden Threat to E-Government", (OECD Policy Brief 2001) set out some key lessons.

- There can be intrinsic **problems with the technology** being deployed. The conventional answer here is to reduce risk by using standard, open market off-the-shelf products. In government environments, funding pressures and complexity in operating environments mean that continuing levels of customisation are required, increasing risk and costs.

- A related issue regards a potential **first mover disadvantage** in implementing elements of the necessary infrastructure, or making policy judgements on which way to progress. Measures such as authentication gateways and public key infrastructures may be seen as essential to advanced integrated transactional services, but they are relatively new and untried in broad e-government applications.

- The much stated "think big, start small, scale fast" doctrine can be difficult to implement because of **ongoing budget scrutiny**. Scaling fast, in particular, may be victim to deferral or cutback. Funding of infrastructure and its upgrading is always easier to defer than more pressing policy imperatives, and unfortunately it can take a crisis such as a failure in service delivery to bring forward the necessary funds, which are then spent in a charged, pressured environment. Governments are not very fast in making decisions on funding, with annual funding cycles the common approach.

- Similarly, the need for a broader vision and related funding to integrate online service delivery into a broader service channel framework can be sacrificed in order to **keep immediate costs down**, or due to the difficulty in challenging existing work practices.

- Implementation can be **too complex**. At one level, the web of government regulations around ICT procurement, industry support, contract requirements, compliance with (often valid) security and other standards can increase costs and drag out implementation timetables. Unfortunately, implementing seamless government services involving a number of agencies unavoidably adds to the complexity of implementation; it is understandable that ICT implementers within agencies can feel more comfortable working alone.

● Project timetables and required deliverables are often subject to **detailed political scrutiny**. Clearly ministerial setting of outcomes and timelines is legitimate. The idea that ICT use is a technical issue and somehow not appropriate for what is seen as political interference is unrealistic and not compatible with the focus now placed on e-government activities. However problems arise when timetables become unrealistic and expectations grow.

● Breaching individual **privacy** has the potential to derail the best e-government plans. Ensuring e-government initiatives are in step with society's expectations in this area is crucial as a means of building trust that privacy will be protected.

● Assuming the perils of implementation have been safely addressed, **take up** can be a major issue. Lower than anticipated levels of use of an online service will lead to criticism that expenditure has been wasted, that expected efficiency gains have not been realised. Higher level of use can lead to rapid declines in service quality as service providers become overburdened. For example more users may lead to an inability to respond to online queries within acceptable timeframes.

Notes

1. This model for electronic service delivery was developed by the Australian National Audit Office and the Australian Office for Government Online. It is available in the Audit Report No. 18, 1999-2000: *Electronic Service Delivery, including Internet Use, by Commonwealth Government Agencies*. See: *www.anao.gov.au*

2. An example is the eEurope report, *Web-based Survey on Electronic Public Services* (2002), which makes a distinction between interaction, two-way interaction and transaction. Stage 4 in this model is then equivalent to stage 3 in the model used above; data sharing is not included in the eEurope model. The Office of the e-Envoy, on the other hand, redefines the model used above so that stage 3 is two-way interaction while stage 4 is still defined as data sharing (Office of e-Envoy. 2000, *Benchmarking Electronic Service Delivery*. 2000)

3. Recent work has reviewed the experience of OECD countries with online engagement, drawing upon the definitions, terms and guiding principles proposed in the *Citizens as Partners* (2001e) report. Undertaken in 2002, this review was conducted as part of the OECD E-Government Project under the auspices of the OECD Expert Group on Government Relations with Citizens and Civil Society, whose members provided significant guidance in defining its scope and submitting country case studies.

4. Section taken from PUMA Policy Brief No. 8, "The Hidden Threat to E-Government: Avoiding large government IT failures" (March 2001)

150

ISBN 92-64-10117-9
The E-Government Imperative
© OECD 2003

Chapter 5

Conclusions and Future Challenges

Implementing e-government has certainly created challenges for member countries, in spite of a long tradition of ICT use in government. While the level of practical experience to draw on when implementing Internet-based applications is now extensive, a range of future challenges will put pressure on public administrations and on e-government programmes to be more responsive, to deliver government priorities more effectively and to do so with fewer resources. This Chapter draws together the project's conclusions and identifies future challenges and priorities for action.

5.1. Conclusions

The impact of e-government at the broadest level is simply better government. E-government can act as an enabler to achieve better policy outcomes, higher quality services, greater engagement with citizens and improve back office procedures. Governments and public administrations will, and should, continue to be judged against these traditional, established criteria for success.

One of the biggest challenges to implementing e-government is the **need for a seamless approach** to serving citizens and businesses. A seamless approach implies a common vision, a common delivery strategy, and numerous back-office changes including organisational change, cooperation and collaboration. Problems with collaboration in public administrations reflect, in part, their compartmentalised structure and the absence of incentives for co-operation. A seamless approach can take many forms, but at a minimum necessitates the establishing of inter-linkages among government agencies in order to provide a common, simple interface for citizens and business.

As outlined in the report, implementation of e-government requires action and change at many levels if it is to succeed in maximising potential benefits. A government-wide vision is required, leadership and commitment is needed to translate this vision into reality, and existing barriers in the way public administration operates will need to be overcome. This report identified ten guiding principles as a framework for future action to advance e-government initiatives. These ten guiding principles fit into four broader areas:

- Vision and political will.
- Common frameworks.
- Co-operation.
- Customer focusfocus and responsibility.

THE E-GOVERNMENT IMPERATIVE – ISBN 92-64-10117-9 – © OECD 2003

GUIDING PRINCIPLES FOR SUCCESSFUL E-GOVERNMENT

Vision/political will

1. **Leadership and Commitment:** Leadership and commitment, at both political and administrative levels, are crucial to managing change. Committed leaders are required to deal with disruptive change, to persevere when benefits take time to emerge, to respond when things go wrong, and to establish visions and plans for the future.

2. **Integration:** E-government is an enabler, not an end in itself. It needs to be integrated into broader policy and service delivery goals, broader public management reform processes and broader information society activity.

Common frameworks/co-operation

3. **Inter-agency collaboration:** E-government is most effective when agencies work together in customer-focussed groupings of agencies. Agency managers need to be able to operate within common frameworks to ensure interoperability, maximise implementation efficiency and avoid duplication. Shared infrastructure needs to be developed to provide a framework for individual agency initiatives. Incentives can help encourage collaboration.

4. **Financing:** ICT spending, where appropriate, should be treated as an investment, with consideration of projected streams of returns. E-government requires a level of certainty of future funding to provide sustainability to projects, avoid wasting resources and gain maximum benefit from given funding levels. A central funding programme could help foster innovation and allow for key demonstration projects.

Customer focus

5. **Access:** Governments should pursue policies to improve access to online services. Many advantages of online government information and services are not replicable offline, so that those who lack access will be excluded unless action is taken.

6. **Choice:** Customers should have choice in the method of interacting with government, and the adoption of online services should not reduce choice. A principle of "no wrong door" to access the administration should be adopted. Services should be driven by an understanding of customer needs.

7. **Citizen engagement:** E-government information and services should be of high quality and engage citizens in the policy process. Information quality policies and feedback mechanisms will help maximise the usefulness of information provision and strengthen citizen participation.

8. **Privacy:** E-government should not be delivered at the expense of established expectations of privacy protection, and should be approached with the goal of protecting individual privacy.

Responsibility

9. **Accountability:** E-government can open up government and policy processes and enhance accountability. Accountability arrangements should ensure that it is clear who is responsible for shared projects and initiatives. Similarly, the use of private sector partnerships must not reduce accountability.

10. **Monitoring and evaluation:** Identifying the demand, costs, benefits and impacts of e-government is crucial if momentum is to be sustained. E-government implementers cannot expect support if they cannot articulate potential benefits.

The means of enabling change through e-government is different in OECD countries, reflecting the current stage of e-government development, different political structures and environments, broader approaches to collaboration and access to funding. Precise impacts on public administrations and the way they adapt to incorporate e-government capacity will differ and will continue to evolve.

Taking these caveats into account, increasing e-government activity has broad implications:

● E-government ways of working will become the norm. The issues surrounding e-government (improved services, citizen engagement, organisational change, leadership, co-ordination, collaboration, skills, public-private partnerships, managing risk and monitoring and evaluation) will increasingly determine how public administrations as a whole will need to operate if they are to remain responsive to the pressures and demands on them.

● The need for cross-government architectures and other collaborative arrangements to reduce duplication and ensure efficient use of infrastructure will intensify. It is important to ensure that this does not result in over-centralisation and hinder managerial oversight and initiative.

● In terms of external governance relationships between citizens, businesses and public administrations, the boundaries between public administrations and society are likely to become more open, with a greater flow of information in both directions. Additionally, governments are likely to increase the provision of information to citizens and open up processes, and receive more input and information relating to policy processes and ways of working. The boundaries between public administrations and society are likely to become more blurred as a result of the greater use of private-sector firms and social intermediaries, driven in part by the imperatives of e-government.

● Within public administrations, the boundaries between agencies may similarly become less distinct, with greater information flows and overlapping processes and policies. This, in turn, would affect ways of working and involve a greater focus on customer and policy outcomes, the development of cross-agency teams and more sharing of data on customers and on policy issues.

● More structured knowledge management strategies could facilitate greater information flows within agencies. This would support a greater focus on customers, improve efficiency and develop a greater sense of organisational identity. The broader benefits of cross-agency collaboration will not emerge unless similar activity and change takes place within individual public administration units.

5.2. Future challenges

To date, e-government has enjoyed a level of **political support** in OECD governments, which have seen e-government as a tool to modernise public administration, as a symbol of modernity, as a way of promoting the development of ICT industry and the move to an information society. The initial impressive visible results of e-government activity – the rapid appearance of numerous government Websites, a number of sophisticated transactional services, the development of portals – made support easy to find, especially since additional funding was often not necessary. The next stage of e-government involves the development of hidden infrastructure, joined-up back-office arrangements, higher levels of funding and possibly disruptive changes to public administrations. This next stage is likely to have less appeal. The benefits are also likely to emerge slowly and be less apparent to the outside observer. The collapse of the dot-com bubble has also made e-commerce and e-government less fashionable. The need for leadership and commitment to change will be more than ever indispensable.

The need for e-government initiatives will continue, and in all likelihood increase, in the light of the broader challenges faced by public administrations and governments. To date, governments have been able to introduce e-government services with little disruption to existing structures and ways of operating. However this phase of e-government is nearing its conclusion in many OECD countries, and governments must now focus on more drastic back-office changes, especially regarding **collaboration with a view to seamless service delivery**. In order to be effective, e-government must force co-ordinators to rethink organisational and internal relations within government. The logic of customer-focused, seamless government, and the need to work jointly to ensure interoperability and reduce duplication applies as much across jurisdictions as it does across agencies at the same level of government. This involves a number of issues, including:

- Since their introduction, ICTs have changed how governments operate. As e-government becomes more prevalent, and as its impact on processes becomes more profound as transactional services develop, there is a greater need for **organisational change** to facilitate and maximise its benefits.

- **Partnering with the private and non-profit sectors** will become increasingly important to maximise the benefits of e-government. Major challenges include the specification of outputs, the sharing of risk, accountability arrangements, and managing the relationship between public and private sector partners (including having the necessary skills).

- The growing complexity of the problems to be faced will challenge traditional delivery modes and related **accountability** structures. The impact of decisions taken at supranational level, greater collaboration across jurisdictions and agencies, and the blurred border between private and public sectors in the delivery of government services will in all probability be more strongly felt. This will influence how citizens see government's ability to respond to their concerns and require assessment of accountability structures, including formal parliamentary arrangements, if government is to remain accountable and open. Accountability frameworks should also take into account provision of information and feedback from service users.

- Public administrations will need to continue to develop policies and technical solutions around the key areas of security, authentication and data storage, in order to preserve the **privacy** of individual citizens' data. If not handled correctly, this issue, more than any other, has the potential to undermine support for e-government. Solutions in this area can be contentious, and privacy issues are exacerbated when linked with seamless government initiatives; the linking and matching of separate data holdings in particular heightens concerns.

- The lack of **vertical e-government integration** across different levels of government (e.g. local, regional, national) is a key challenge to the successful implementation of e-government. Users want effective service, and care less about differences in approach and/or responsibility among levels of government. Uncoordinated local initiatives can lead to costly incompatibility or duplication.

- E-government should be a **continuous process of government improvement**, rather than simply putting services online in successive stages. Managing the transition to online service delivery will demand changes in all aspects of the public administration.

- The initial introduction of online services can be expensive when these services are introduced separately from existing traditional service channels. However, the development of online services as part of a service channel strategy, with the opportunity taken to reengineer overall service delivery processes, provides the means to capture overall efficiencies and savings

- OECD countries have difficulty **monitoring and evaluating** e-government (including cost, benefit, and level of demand), yet increased support for e-government projects will be dependent on these measures. Monitoring and evaluation should be used effectively for programme improvement and targeting, and needs to be better tied to e-government planning.

Citizens are interested not only in the provision of services online, but also in the opportunities ICT presents to **increase citizen engagement** in the policy process. Governments will need to create new and more direct links with civil society to improve the quality and responsiveness of decision-making. But citizens' enhanced ability to communicate directly with public administrations may put elected representatives in danger of being bypassed.

In short, e-government will affect the relationship between parliament, the executive and citizens, challenging traditional concepts of political legitimacy, representation and ministerial accountability. These changes will make striking a balance between the representative and participatory models of democracy important.

5.3. Priorities for action

This report has argued that there is a need to take action to ensure that the benefits of e-government activity are maximised. Action is needed because the initial attraction of e-government has worn off in many countries just when e-government initiatives are starting to mature and to deliver major benefits. In order to deliver benefits, e-government will increasingly disrupt ways of working, require increased infrastructure investment and face increasing customer expectations. Additionally, the implementation of e-government initiatives needs to become as efficient and effective as possible, as reliance and expenditure on ICT increases.

The broad, cross-sector nature of e-government and the increasing number of service partners both within and outside of government demand public governance frameworks that take into consideration all e-government functions from a whole-of-government perspective. Such frameworks serve to diffuse the overall vision throughout government and to show all stakeholders (from heads of agencies to frontline service deliverers) their role in support of the overall process. They are necessary to ensure accountability for service quality when multiple agencies are providing seamless services. They allow internal input and feedback into the e-government policy development process, ensuring ownership of e-government vision and goals. And they help to correct policies along the way and to capture unintended benefits. The following checklist, based on the OECD Guiding Principles for Successful E-Government, presents a list of questions that e-government leaders should ask themselves as they introduce, develop and strengthen e-government initiatives.

In terms of **international co-operation**, considerable co-operation takes place through organisations such as the ICA[1] and the GOL-IN.[2] In addition to the present project, the OECD is active through the Working Party on the Information Economy (WPIE), the Working Party on Indicators for the Information Society (WPIIS) and the Working Party on Information Security and Privacy (WPISP). Further areas where sharing experience to address common issues could be valuable include:

- Co-operation on architecture frameworks for better use of ICT in government.
- Further co-operation on efforts to measure demand, costs and benefits for e-government initiatives.

CHECKLIST FOR SUCCESSFUL E-GOVERNMENT

Vision/political will

1. **Leadership and commitment:**

   - Do you have the necessary leadership and commitment at the political level in order to develop an e-government vision and guide change over the long term?

   - Is there leadership and commitment at the administrative level to implement change?

2. **Integration:**

   - Has there been a review of barriers to e-government implementation?

   - Is e-government integrated into broader policy and service delivery goals and processes?

   - Is e-government integrated into public management reform goals and processes?

   - Is e-government integrated into broader information society activity?

Common frameworks/co-operation

3. **Inter-agency collaboration:**

   - Are agencies working together in customer-focussed groupings of agencies?

   - Are agency managers operating within common frameworks to ensure interoperability, maximise implementation efficiency and avoid duplication?

   - Does shared infrastructure exist to provide a framework for individual agency initiatives?

   - Are there incentives to help encourage collaboration and seamless service delivery?

4. **Financing:**

   - Can ICT spending, where appropriate, be treated as an investment with consideration of projected streams of returns?

   - Is there a degree of certainty of future funding in order to provide sustainability to projects (and thus gain maximum benefit from given funding levels and avoid wasting resources)?

   - Are there programmes (such as a central funding programme) to help foster innovation and allow for key demonstration projects?

Customer focus

5. **Access:**

   - Is the government pursuing policies to improve access to online services?

THE E-GOVERNMENT IMPERATIVE – ISBN 92-64-10117-9 – © OECD 2003

CHECKLIST FOR SUCCESSFUL E-GOVERNMENT (*cont.*)

6. **Choice:**

   - Do customers have choice in the method of interacting with government?
   - Is there a "no wrong door" principle for accessing the administration?
   - Are services driven by an understanding of customer needs?

7. **Citizen engagement:**

   - Does e-government engage citizens in the policy process?
   - Are there information quality policies and feedback mechanisms in place to help maximise the usefulness of information provision and strengthen citizen participation?

8. **Privacy:**

   - Are there mechanisms in place to protect individual privacy with regard to e-government?
   - Do broad standards for privacy protection allow for information sharing between agencies while preventing abuse?

Responsibility

9. **Accountability:**

   - Do accountability arrangements ensure that it is clear who is responsible for shared projects and initiatives?
   - Does the use of private sector partnerships maintain levels of accountability?

10. **Monitoring and evaluation:**

   - Is there a framework in place to identify the demand, costs, benefits and impact of e- government?
   - Are e-government implementers able to articulate and demonstrate the benefits of e- government in order to raise support for their projects?

- Harmonisation of policies for data sharing across countries (for example regarding security and privacy).

   The OECD will remain active in the international e-government arena.

Notes

1. International Council for Information Technology in Government Administration *www.ica-it.org/*

2. Government Online International Network *www.governments-online.org*

Bibliography

ALLEN, B., JUILLET, L., MINOOSEPEHR, S., PAQUET, G. and ROY, J. (2002), "E-Government and Collaboration: Structural, Accountability and Cultural Reform".

BJÖRKQVIST, S. (2002), "Experiences with e-Government in Statistics Finland".

BOVAIRD, T. (2002a), "Performance Measurement and Evaluation of e-Government and e-Governance Programmes and Initiatives".

BOVAIRD, T. (2002b), "E-Government and Organisational Change: New Ways of Linking the Front and Back Offices of Government Departments, Government Agencies and Local Government".

CHATILLON, G. (2002), "Confidence in E-Government: The Outlook for a Legal Framework for Personal Data and Privacy".

CLIFT, S. (2003), "Public Net-Work: Online Information Exchange in the Pursuit of Public Service Goals".

CULBERTSON, S. (2002a), "E-Government and Organisational Change".

CULBERTSON, S. (2002b), "Transformed Government: Case Studies on the Impact of E-government in Public Administrations".

CORSI, M. and GULLO, E. (2002), "Measuring E-Government in Italy".

CZERNIAWSKI, S. (2002), "Measuring E-Government in the United Kingdom".

FINE, E. (2002), "A Community-Based Approach to Preparing for Change in the Workplace".

FINN, B. and GIOVANNINI, E. (forthcoming), "Statistical Developments and Strategies in the Context of e-Government".

FRISSEN, V. (2002), "The e-mancipation of the Citizen and the Future of e-government: Reflections on ICT and Citizens' Partnership".

GARTNER RESEARCH (2002), "The Gartner Framework for E-Government Strategy Assessment".

GBDe (Global Business Dialogue on Electronic Commerce) 2002, "E-Government".

GOVERNMENT ON-LINE CANADA (2002), "Annual Report on Canada's Progress 2002", *www.gol-ged.ca*

HARVARD POLICY GROUP ON NETWORK-ENABLED SERVICES AND GOVERNMENT (2001), "Improving Budgeting and Financing for Promising IT Initiatives".

HOLLAND, C., BONGERS, F., VANDEBERG, R., KELLER, W. and TE VELDE, R. (2002), "Building Blocks and Recommendations for a Standardised Measuring Tool".

HOLMES, D. (2002a), "Marketing e-Government".

HOLMES, D. (2002b), "E-Government Case Studies".

HOPKINS, A. (2002), "Discussion paper on the issue of responsive e-government services from the perspective of service users".

IDA (Interchange of Data between Administrations) (2002), Transborder e-procurement Study "Public eProcurement: Analysis of Public e-procurement Initiatives", Summary Report *http://europa.eu.int.*

KERSCHOT, H. and POTÉ, K. (2001), "Web-based Survey on Electronic Public Services (Results of the first measurement: October 2001)".

LENIHAN, D. G. (2002), "Realigning Governance: From E-Government To E-Democracy".

MACINTOSH, A. (2002), "Using information and communication technologies to enhance citizen engagement in the policy process".

MELE, V. (2002), "Paradigm and Practice: the Innovative Organisation".

MONTAGNIER, W., MULLER, E. and VICKERY, G. (2002), "The Digital Divide: Diffusion and Use of ICTs".

MURPHY, M. (2002), "Organisational Change and Firm Performance".

National Audit Office (NAO) (2002), "Better Services through e-government: Case Studies in Support of Better Public Services through e-government".

OECD (2000), *Government of the Future*, OECD, Paris.

OECD (2001a), *The Electronic Commerce Business Impacts Project* (EBIP), Paris.

OECD (2001b), *Public Sector Leadership for the 21st Century*, Paris.

OECD (2001c), *Understanding the Digital Divide*, Paris.

OECD (2001d), *Communication Outlook*, Paris.

OECD (2001e), *Citizens as Partners: Information, Consultation and Public Participation in Policy Making*, Paris.

OECD (2001f), *The New Economy: Beyond the Hype*, Paris.

OECD Policy Brief (2001), The Hidden Threat to E-Government.

OECD (2002a), *Information Technology Outlook*, Paris.

OECD (2002b), *Measuring the Information Economy*, Paris.

OECD (2003a), *E-Government in Finland*, Paris.

OECD (2003b), *Promises and Problems of E-Democracy: Challenges of Online Citizen Engagement*, Paris.

OECD (forthcoming), *From In-line to Online: Delivering Better Services*, Paris.

PARRADO DIEZ, S. (2002), "ICT Related Skills for E-Government".

POLAND, P. (2001), "Online Consultation in GOL Countries, Initiatives to Foster E-Democracy". The Government Online International Network.

REEDER, F. S. and PANDY, S. M. (2002), "Identifying Effective Funding Models for E-Government".

ROY, J., ALLEN, B. and LIFSHITZ, A. (2002), "E-Government and Private-Public Partnerships: Relational Challenges and Strategic Directions".

SETTLES, A. (2002), "What Skills are Needed in an E-World: E-Government Skills and Training Programmes for the Public Sector?".

SØRGAARD, P. (2002), "Implementing E-Government: Leadership and Co-ordination".

STATSKONTORET (Swedish Agency for Public Management) (2000), "The 24/7 Agency; Criteria for 24/7 Agencies in the Networked Public Administration", Stockholm.

WORLD ECONOMIC FORUM (in association with INSEAD and infoDEV), (2002-2003), "The Global Information Technology Report".

WORLD MARKETS RESEARCH CENTRE (2001), "Global E-Government Survey".

VAN DUIVENBODEN, H. (2002), "Citizen Participation in Public Administration: The Impact of Citizen Oriented Public Services on Government and Citizen".

VAN GILS, D. (2002), "Evaluation Practices used by OECD Member Countries to Assess E-Government".

Country Papers

Australia Country Paper (2002a), "Public-Private Partnerships".

Australia Country Paper (2002b), "A case study on collaboration: The development of an Information Technology Architecture and Governance policy framework for federal agencies".

Australia Country Paper (2002c), "Interoperability through collaboration".

Canada Country Paper (2002a), "Government On-Line Investment Strategies: the Canadian Example".

Canada Country Paper (2002b), "Evaluating at the Agency Level: E-Government Capacity Check".

Canada Country Paper (2002c), "A Community-Based Approach to Preparing for Change in the Workplace".

Denmark Country Paper (2002), "E-Government the Danish way: A tight link between eGovernment, Regulatory and Administrative Regulation".

Finland Country Paper (2002), "Private–public partnerships in e-Government service delivery".

France Country Paper (2002), "Développement de l'administration électronique: L'expérience française".

Germany Country Paper (2002a), "Implementing E-Government: Leadership and Co-ordination".

Germany Country Paper (2002b), "BundOnline 2005: Challenges to Collaboration".

Italy Country Paper (2002a), "Financial aspects of e-government implementation in Italy".

Italy Country Paper (2002b), "A Network of Regional Competence Centres (RCC) to Support Collaboration among Italian Public Administrations in the Development of E-Government".

Japan Country Paper (2002a), "Leadership and Co-ordination".

Japan Country Paper (2002b), "E-government skills in Japan".

Korea Country Paper (2002a), "Leadership and Co-ordination in E-Government: A case study of South Korea".

Korea Country Paper (2002b), "Skills for Implementing eGovernment Policy: eGovernment Project for Local Governments in Korea".

United States Country Paper (2002a), "United States' Experience with Public-Private Partnerships: Elements of Effective Public-*Purpose* Partnerships".

United States Country Paper (2002b), "Building the E-Government Workforce".

ANNEX I

Glossary

This glossary was compiled for the purpose of this study, and describes how the terms are used in this report.

ACTIVE PARTICIPATION – A relation based on partnership with government, in which citizens actively engage in the policy-making process. It acknowledges a role for citizens in proposing policy options and shaping the policy dialogue – although the responsibility for the final decision or policy formulation rests with the government.

AUTHENTICATION – A security measure for checking a user's identity before being allowed Internet or intranet access, typically by entering a user identity and/or password.

BACK OFFICE – The internal operations of an organisation that support core processes and are not accessible or visible to the general public.

EXTERNAL BARRIERS – External barriers to e-government are obstacles need to be resolved with the help of other actors (*e.g.* in central administrations) in order to be overcome. They often concern breakdowns, missing components or lack of flexibility in the government-wide frameworks that enable e-government. The result is often the inability to achieve a whole-of-government or seamless perspective in e-government implementation.

CHANNELS – A means of accessing services (*e.g.* Internet, telephone, visit to a government office). Different types of customers use different service access channels

CONSULTATION – A two-way relationship between the citizen and government, in which governments consult citizens and ask for their feedback and citizens provide feedback to government. Governments define the issues for consultation, set the questions and manage the process, while citizens are invited to contribute their views and opinions.

E-GOVERNMENT – The use of information and communication technologies (ICTs), and particularly the Internet, as a tool to achieve better government.

E-GOVERNMENT ACTIVITIES – Is broadly used to cover all activities relating to the use of ICTs by governments. It thus covers both an agency's activities with regard to citizens, businesses and other public agencies, as well as activities concerning internal administration processes, structures and behaviour.

FRONT OFFICE – Refers to government as its constituents see it, meaning the information and service providers, and the interaction between government and both citizens and business.

INFORMATION – A one-way relation in which government produces and delivers information for use by citizens. It covers both "passive" access to information upon demand from citizens and "active" measures by government to **disseminate** information to citizens.

INFORMATION AND COMMUNICATIONS TECHNOLOGY (ICT) – Refers to both computer and communication technology. IT (information technology) is defined as any equipment or interconnected system (subsystem) of equipment that includes all forms of technology used to create, store, manipulate, manage, move, display, switch, interchange, transmit or receive information in its various forms. Information can be in the form of: business data; voice conversations; still images; motion pictures; multimedia presentations and other forms including those not yet conceived. The meaning of communication refers to a system of shared symbols and meanings that binds people together into a group, a community, or a culture. The word communication was added to IT so as to make a network of the usage of Information Technology.[1]

INFORMATION MANAGEMENT (IM) – Operations which develop and maintain the information reserves and information processes of an organisation.

INFORMATION NETWORK – A system of IT hardware and services which provides users with delivery and retrieval services in a given area (*e.g.* electronic mail, directories and video services);

INFORMATION NETWORK INFRASTRUCTURE – The whole system of transmission links, access procedures, legal and general frameworks, and the basic and supportive services of the information network;

INFORMATION SOCIETY (IS) – A society which makes extensive use of information networks and ICT, produces large quantities of information and communications products and services, and has a diversified content industry.

INFORMATION TECHNOLOGY (IT) – Means the hardware, software and methods used for the automatic processing and transfer of data.

1. Adapted from *http://afrinet.intnet.mu/competition2002/rcpl2/ict/frameless/definition.htm*

INTEROPERABILITY – The ability for organisations to share information and data (*e.g.* by using common standards).

MIDDLEWARE – Middleware is software that integrates services and distributed applications across the Internet or local area networks, and may provide a set of services such as authentication, messaging, transactions, etc. Middleware allows government organisations to share data between front office service delivery channels and back offices applications and processes, and is increasingly perceived as a technology for delivery of joined-up e-government services.

NO WRONG DOOR POLICY – Means keeping a variety of service access channels operational (government offices, telephone call centres, government websites) so that citizens can choose and use their preferred mode of access. See also "channel". (Note that in Canada, "no wrong door" policy refers to Internet channels only, and means that no matter which website or portal is accessed, users can link to all other government websites and portals.)

ONE-STOP SHOP – A government office where services by multiple public administration authorities are available on the same visit.

ONLINE GOVERNMENT SERVICES – Services provided by, but not necessarily supplied by, the public administration to citizens, businesses and organisations as well as to other public administration units through information networks.

PORTAL – This is a dedicated service that co-ordinates and presents information and services from different, independent suppliers into one interface, typically a website. The information is categorised in accordance with given criteria related to users' needs.

PUBLIC ACCESS TERMINAL – A PC with Internet access installed in a public space such as a library, available for free use by the public.

PUBLIC KEY INFRASTRUCTURE (PKI) – PKI is a method for authenticating a message sender or encrypting a message. It enables users of an insecure public network, such as the Internet, to securely and privately exchange data through the use of a public and a private cryptographic key pair that is obtained and shared through a trusted authority. It provides for a *digital certificate* that can identify an individual or an organisation and directory services that can store and, when necessary, revoke the certificates.

SEAMLESS SERVICES – This means presenting easy to use, function-driven services to the public. Seamless services provide citizens with what they need to know in a particular topic or client grouping, without having to know which government level or agency they must contact to get it. It provides all the information and services a user needs in one website.

ANNEX II

E-Government Statistics

This annex provides e-government statistics from selected OECD countries.

Figure 3. **Online availability of public services (2001-2002)**

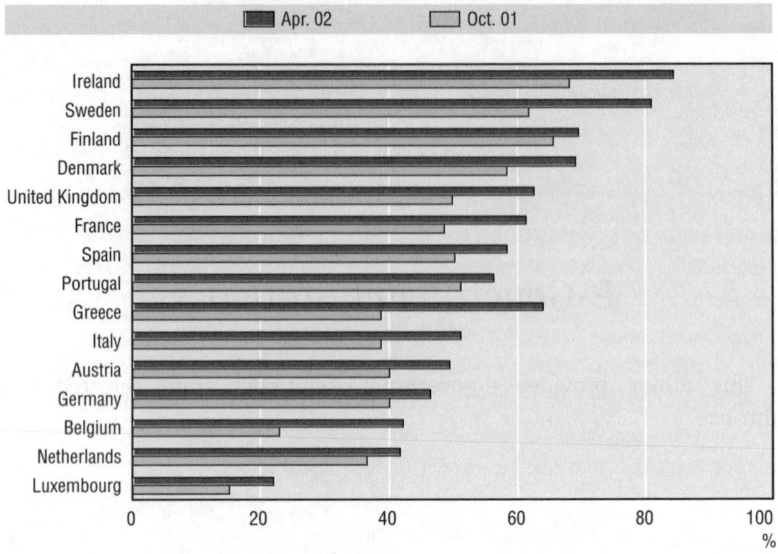

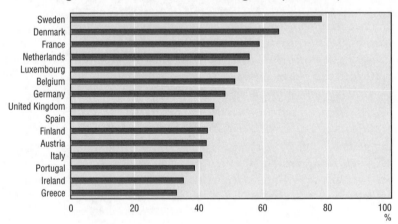

Source: eEurope.

Figure 4. **Per cent of users visiting sites (June 2002)**

Source: eEurope.

Figure 5. **Per cent of national sites offering online services**

Percentage of websites in each country that have each feature covered in the survey, such as online services, publications and databases

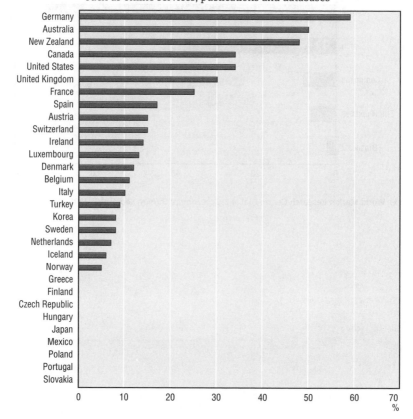

Source: World Market Research Centre Global E-Government Survey, September 2001.

Figure 6. **Per cent of government websites offering public outreach (survey of 196 nations)**

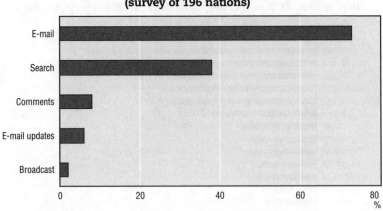

Source: World Market Research Centre Global E-Government Survey, September 2001.

THE E-GOVERNMENT IMPERATIVE – ISBN 92-64-10117-9 – © OECD 2003

Figure 7. **Government services online**

Are government services (downloadable permit applications, tax payments, government tenders) available on the Internet in your country:
1 = not available; 7 = commonly available

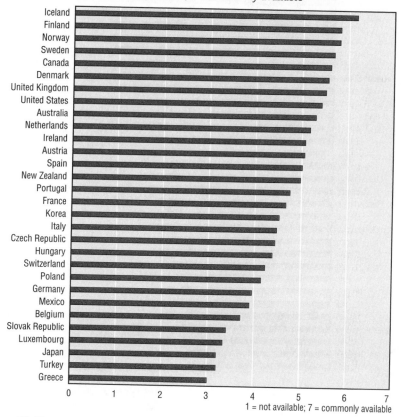

1 = not available; 7 = commonly available

Source: World Economic Forum, "The Global Information Technology Report" (2002-2003).

Figure 8. **Government success in ICT promotion**

Government programs promoting the use of ICT are:
1 not very successful; 7 = highly successful

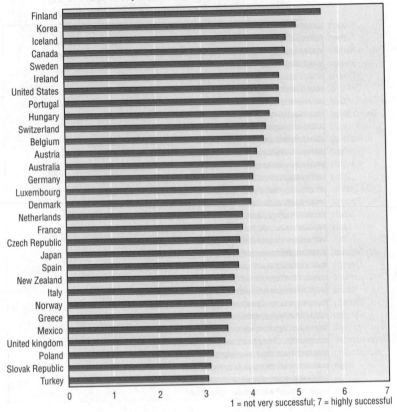

Source: World Economic Forum, "The Global Information Technology Report" (2002-2003).

THE E-GOVERNMENT IMPERATIVE – ISBN 92-64-10117-9 – © OECD 2003

Figure 9. **Government prioritization of ICT**

ICT are an overall priority for the government:
1 = strongly disagree; 7 = strongly agree

Finland							
Japan							
Sweden							
Ireland							
Hungary							
United States							
Korea							
Canada							
Iceland							
Luxembourg							
Germany							
Switzerland							
Denmark							
Spain							
United Kingdom							
Czech Republic							
Portugal							
Netherlands							
Austria							
Belgium							
Mexico							
France							
Australia							
Norway							
Italy							
New Zealand							
Greece							
Slovak Republic							
Turkey							
Poland							

0   1   2   3   4   5   6   7

1 = strongly disagree; 7 = strongly agree

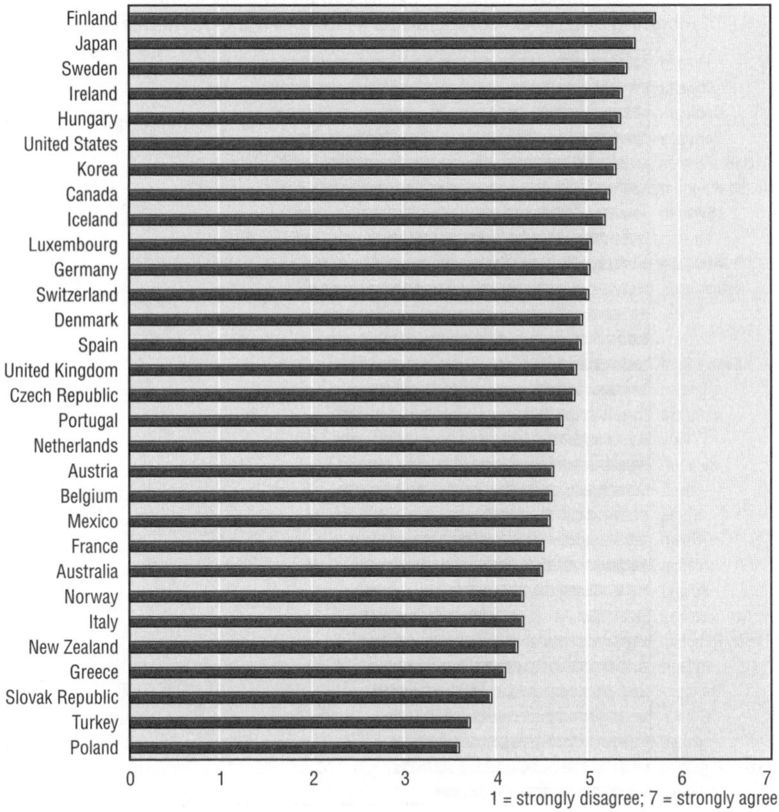

Source: World Economic Forum, "The Global Information Technology Report" (2002-2003).

Figure 10. **Use of Internet-based transactions with government (businesses)**

Please rate your company's position in Internet-based interactions with government *versus* international competitors in its largest business:
1 = behind other local companies; 5 = equal to the best in the world

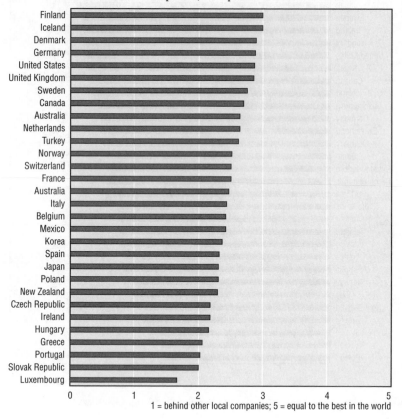

1 = behind other local companies; 5 = equal to the best in the world

Source: World Economic Forum, "The Global Information Technology Report" (2002-2003).

THE E-GOVERNMENT IMPERATIVE – ISBN 92-64-10117-9 – © OECD 2003

Figure 11. **Competence of public officials**

The competence level of personnel in the civil service is:
1 = lower than the private sector; 7 = higher than the private sector

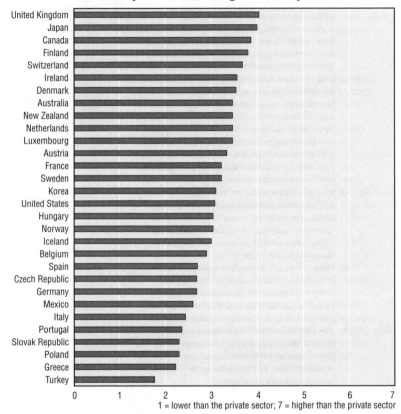

1 = lower than the private sector; 7 = higher than the private sector

Source: World Economic Forum, "The Global Information Technology Report" (2002-2003).

Figure 12. **Government procurement of advanced technology**

Government purchase decisions for the procurement of advanced technology are:
1 = based solely on price; 7 = based on technology and encourage innovation

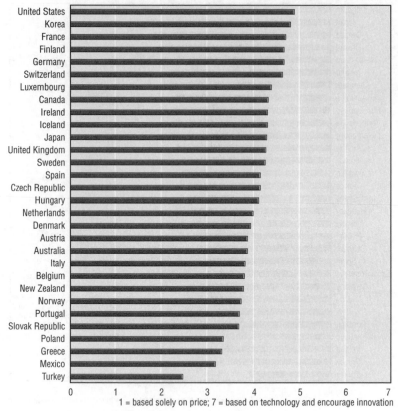

1 = based solely on price; 7 = based on technology and encourage innovation

Source: World Economic Forum, "The Global Information Technology Report" (2002-2003).

Figure 13. **Internet and e-mail access in Canada's public and private sectors, 2000**

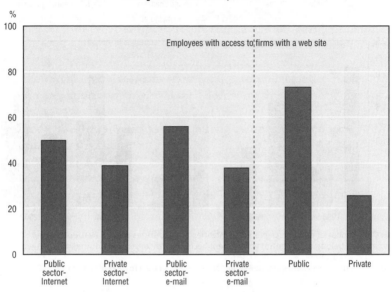

Source: Statistics Canada (2001), "Electronic Commerce and Technology Use", Connectedness Series, Ottawa, September.

Figure 14. **Government Internet access and websites in Australia, 1997/98**

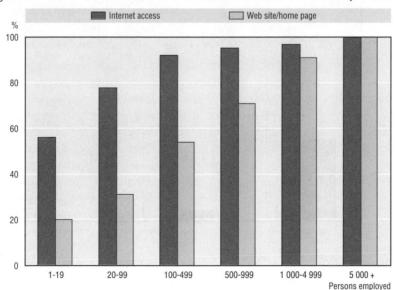

Source: Australian Bureau of Statistics (1999), "Government Use of Information Technology", 8119.0, Canberra.

Figure 15. **Employees per PC in Japan's central government, FY 1998-2002**

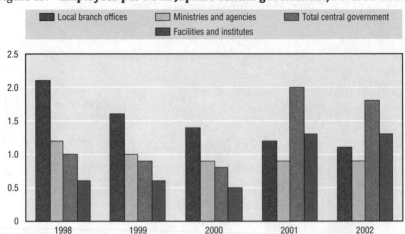

Note: The number of employees per PC in facilities and institutes rose in 2001 due to over 50 national organisations belonging to central government becoming "Incorporated Administrative Agency" not in the central government.
Source: Administrative Management Bureau, Basic Survey on the Progress of Government ICT Use, Tokyo.

Figure 16. **ICT use in the Finnish government, 1995 and 2000**

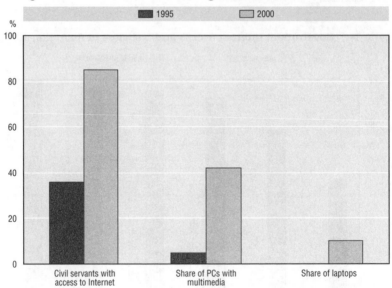

Source: Statistics Finland (2001), On the Road to the Finnish Information Society III, Helsinki.

Figure 17. **Personal Internet usage by purpose in the UK, July 2000**

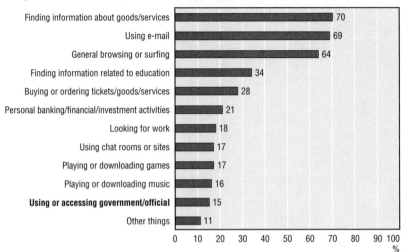

Note: Adult access to the Internet for personal use. Percentages do not add up to 100 as respondents may give more than one answer.
Source: UK National Statistics, 26 September 2000.

ANNEX III

ICT Diffusion and the Digital Divide

This statistical annex provides data on ICT diffusion in selected OECD countries.

Figure 18. **Fixed telecommunication access channels in OECD countries**

Per 100 inhabitants (1990, 1995 and 1999)

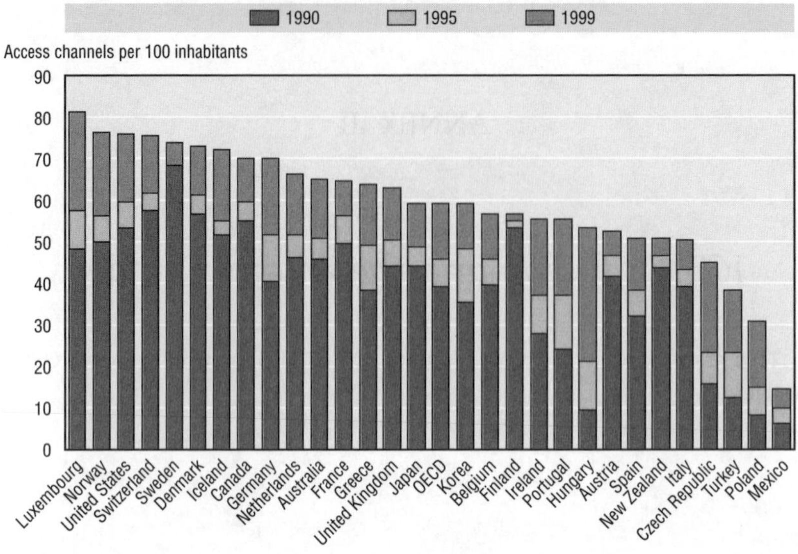

■ 1990   □ 1995   ■ 1999

Access channels per 100 inhabitants

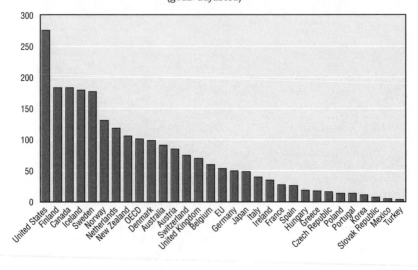

Source: OECD Communications Outlook (2001d).

Figure 19. **Internet hosts in OECD countries per 1 000 inhabitants, July 2001**

(gTLD adjusted)

Source: OECD, from Netsizer (www.netsizer.com).

Figure 20. **Secure servers per million inhabitants, July 2001**

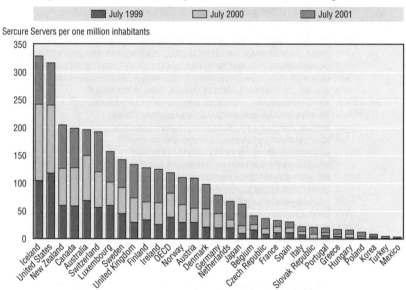

Source: OECD (*www.oecd.org/sti/telecom*) based on Netcraft (*www.netcraft.com*).

Figure 21. **Access to a home computer in selected OECD countries, 1994-2001**

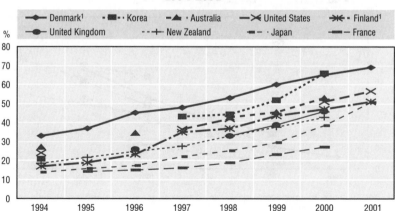

1. First quarter for 2001.
Source: OECD, ICT database, December 2001.

Figure 22. **Households with access to a home computer, 2000 and 2001**

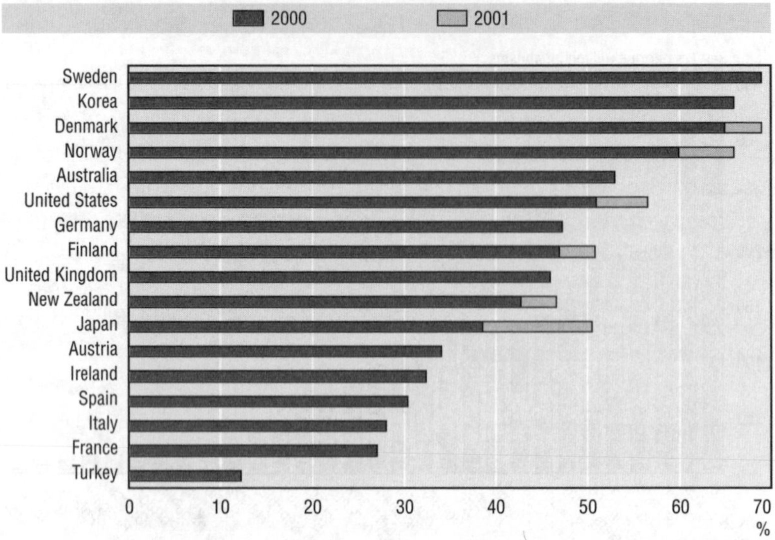

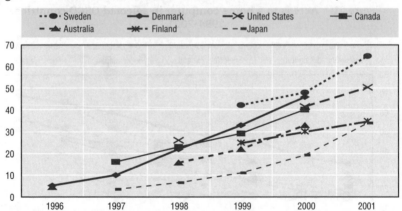

Source: OECD Science, Technology and Industry Scoreboard (2001), ICT database, March 2002.

Figure 23. **Household access to Internet in selected countries, 1996-2001**

Note: For Denmark, Internet access via a home computer; for other countries access via any device (computer, phone, TV, etc.).
Source: OECD, ICT database, September 2001.

THE E-GOVERNMENT IMPERATIVE – ISBN 92-64-10117-9 – © OECD 2003

Figure 24. **Households with access to Internet, 2000 and 2001**

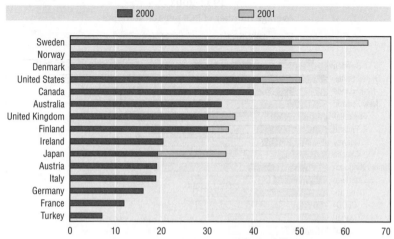

Note: For Denmark, Ireland and the United Kingdom, access to the Internet via a home computer; for the other countries access to the Internet through any device (*e.g.* computer, phone, TV, etc.)
Source: *OECD Science, Technology and Industry Scoreboard* (2001).

Figure 25. **Diffusion of information technology in the education system, 1992-2001**

Average number of PCs per 100 students

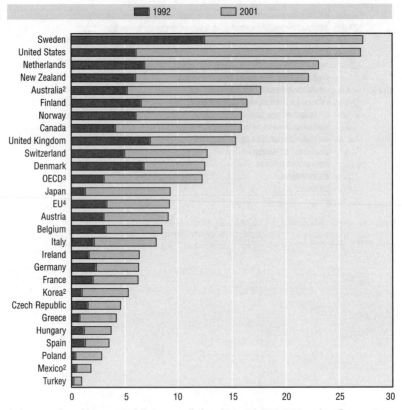

1. Average number of PCs per 100 full-time enrolled students. For 2001, 1999 student figures were used.
2. 1993.
3. Estimates for 1992. OECD excluding Portugal, the Slovak Republic and Luxembourg.
4. Estimates for 1992. EU excluding Portugal and Luxembourg.
Source: OECD, based on World Information Technology and Services Alliance (WITSA)/International Data Corporation (IDC), 2002.

Figure 26. **OECD Internet access basket for 40 hours at peak times using discounted PSTN rates**

USD, PPP, including VAT (August 2001)

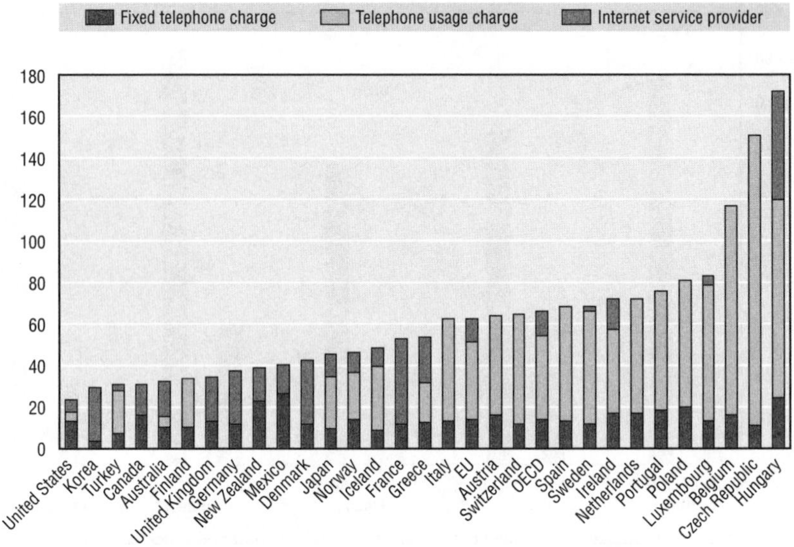

Note: Internet access costs differ substantially between OECD countries, primarily due to differences in variable telephone charges and the costs of Internet service providers. Previous OECD studies show that these differences are primarily due to the state of competition in different member countries.
Source: OECD.

Figure 27. **PC penetration by household income for selected OECD countries, 2000**

Percentages

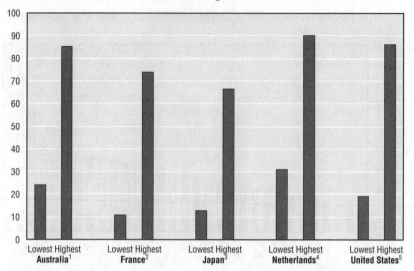

Note: Because of differences in income brackets used, data is not comparable across countries.
1. Lowest income bracket: less than AUD 25 000; highest income bracket: more than AUD 100 000.
2. Lowest income bracket: less than FRF 80 000; highest income bracket: more than FRF 450 000.
3. Lowest income bracket: less than JPY 3 million; highest income bracket: more than JPY 12 million.
4. Lowest income bracket: second income decile (the second decile is used because lowest income decile includes students who have generally higher ICT penetration rates); highest income bracket: tenth income decile.
5. Lowest income bracket: less than USD 15 000; highest income bracket: more than USD 75 000. US data for 2001 shows an increase to 89.0% for the highest income bracket, and 23.8% for the lowest income bracket.

Source: OECD, based on data from Australian Bureau of Statistics, INSEE, Japanese Economic Planning Agency, Statistics Netherlands, and US Bureau of Census.

Figure 28. **Internet access by household income for selected OECD countries, 2000**

Percentages

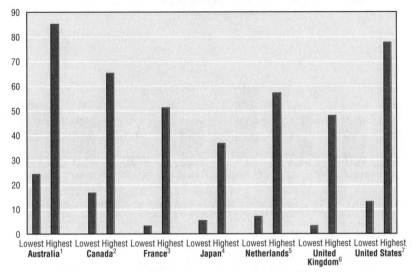

Lowest Highest Lowest Highest Lowest Highest Lowest Highest Lowest Highest Lowest Highest Lowest Highest
Australia[1] **Canada**[2] **France**[3] **Japan**[4] **Netherlands**[5] **United Kingdom**[6] **United States**[7]

Note: Because of differences in income brackets used, data is not comparable across countries.
1. Lowest income bracket: less than AUD 25 000; highest income bracket: more than AUD 100 000.
2. Percentage of households having regular use of the computer from home. Lowest income bracket: first income quartile; highest income bracket: fourth income quartile.
3. Lowest income bracket: less than FRF 80 000; highest income bracket: more than FRF 450 000.
4. Lowest income bracket: less than JPY 3 million; highest income bracket: more than JPY 12 million.
5. 1999; lowest income bracket: second income decile (the second decile is used because lowest income decile includes students who have generally higher ICT penetration rates); highest income bracket: tenth income decile.
6. Smallest income bracket: second decile of income; Highest income bracket: Tenth income decile.
7. Lowest income bracket: less than USD 15 000; highest income bracket: more than USD 75 000. US data for 2001 shows an increase to 85.4% for the highest income bracket, and 17.7% for the lowest income bracket.
Source: OECD, based on national statistics.

Figure 29. **Internet home access among households by income level***
Percentages, 2000

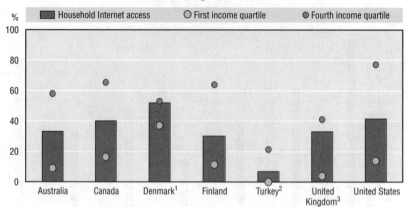

* For Denmark and the United Kingdom, access to the Internet via a home computer; for the other countries access to the Internet through any device (*e.g.* computer, phone, TV, etc.).
1. First quarter 2001.
2. Households in urban areas only.
3. Last quarter 2000.
Source: OECD and national sources.

Figure 30. **PC and Internet access by educational level**
In the United States and the Netherlands (%)

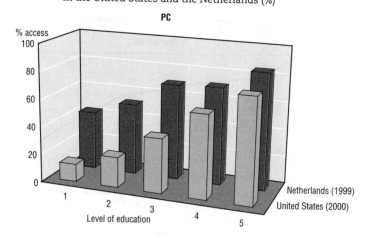

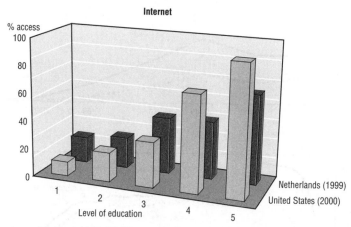

Note: Data apply to the educational attainment of the head of household in the US, the person interviewed in the Netherlands.

Educational levels 1 through 5 are defined as follows:

1. Elementary school in US; primary education in the Netherlands.
2. Some high school in the US; secondary education in the Netherlands.
3. High school diploma or GED in the US; lower general secondary education in the Netherlands.
4. Some college in the US; senior, higher general secondary education/intermediate vocational education/pre-university in the Netherlands.
5. BA or more in the US; higher vocational education/university in the Netherlands.

Source: OECD from national sources.

Figure 31. **PC and Internet penetration rate by age (%)**
Percentages

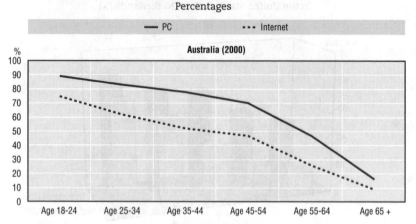

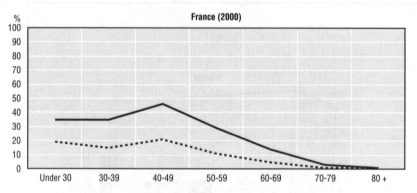

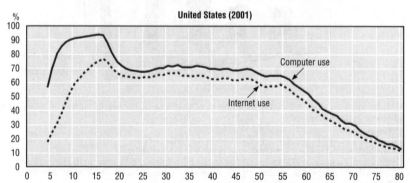

Note: Age of head of household in France. Age of individual in Australia and United States, and includes adults accessing the Internet from any site.
Source: OECD from national statistical sources.

Table 4. **Internet and gender**

Percentages

	1998	1999	2000	2001
Australia				
Male	35	45	50	. .
Female	28	37	43	. .
Total	32	41	47	. .
Norway				
Male	43	53	64	72
Female	33	42	54	65
Total	42	51	63	67
Sweden				
Male	32	. .	67	. .
Female	26	. .	63	. .
Total	29	. .	65	. .
United States				
Male	34	. .	45	54
Female	31	. .	44	54
Total	33	. .	44	54

Note: Individual home access in Sweden and Norway, Internet use from any location in Australia and the United States.
Source: OECD from national statistical sources.

Figure 32. **Urban homes are more connected than rural ones**
Internet access among rural and urban households

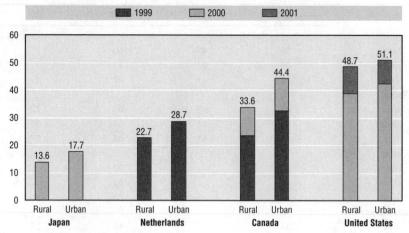

Note: For the Netherlands, "rural" is defined as a low degree of urbanisation, and "urban" a high degree. For Japan, "rural" is defined as "villages and towns" and "urban" as "cities". For both countries, the highest categories were not taken into account. For Canada, urban refers to the top 15 metropolitan areas and rural refers to other households.
Source: OECD, based on national statistical sources.

Figure 33. **English is the main language of the Internet**
Links to secure servers by language (July 2000)

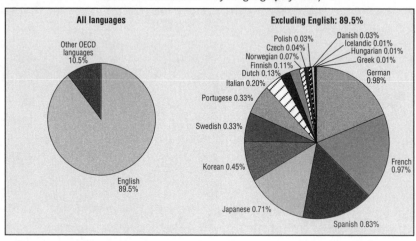

Source: OECD Understanding the Digital Divide (2001c).

Figure 34. **PC access gap by income**
Difference between access rates of highest and lowest income groups

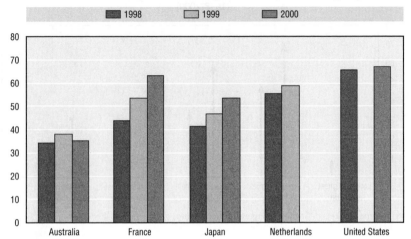

Note: Income groups defined as in Figure 14.
Source: OECD based on national sources.

Figure 35. **Internet access gap by income**
Difference between access rates of highest and lowest income groups

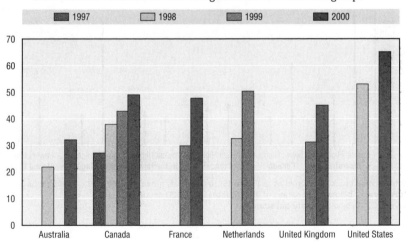

Note: Income groups defined as in Figure 15. Details, including some 2001 data, table on Internet access, below.
Source: OECD based on national sources.

Figure 36. **% growth rate of PCs in households of lowest and highest income levels**

(1998-2000)

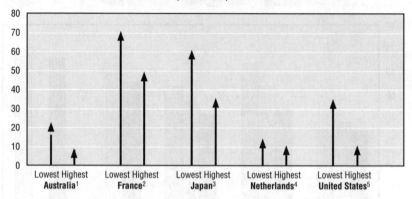

Note: Income brackets defined as in Figure 14. Netherlands growth is 1998-1999.
Source: OECD, based on national sources.

Figure 37. **% growth rate of Internet in households of lowest and highest income levels**

(1998-2000)

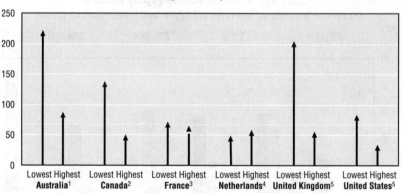

Note: Income brackets defined as in Figure 15. Netherlands growth is 1998-1999. The table on Internet growth rates, below, gives details of growth rates in 9 OECD countries.
Source: OECD, based on national sources.

Table 5. **Households with access to a home computer in selected OECD countries 1986-2001**

	1986	1987	1988	1989	1990	1991	1992	1993	1994	1995	1996	1997	1998	1999	2000	2001
Percentage of households																
Australia[1]									26.9		34.7		42.6	45.3	53.0	
Austria															34.0	
Belgium														45.4		
Canada[2]	10.3			16.2	18.5	20.0	23.0	25.0	28.8	31.6						
Canada[3]												36.4	40.6	50.0		
Denmark				15.0				27.0	33.0	37.0	45.0	48.0	53.0	60.0	65.0	69.0
Finland				8.0					17.0	19.0	23.0	35.0	37.0	43.4	47.0	50.9
France[4]		7.0		8.2			11.0			14.3	15.0	16.0	19.0	23.0	27.0	
Germany														44.9	47.3	
Ireland															32.4	
Italy[5]														29.5	28.1	
Japan[6]		11.7	9.7	11.6	10.6	11.5	12.2	11.9	13.9	15.6	17.3	22.1	25.2	29.5	38.6	50.5
Japan[7]												22.3	28.8	32.6	37.7	
Korea									20.7			43.2	44.5	51.8	66.0	
Mexico[8]														11.1		
New Zealand[9]	6.7	8.6	9.6	11.5	11.6	13.3	15.9	17.1	18.6	21.7	24.8	27.6	32.9	37.5	42.8	46.6
Norway														60.0	66.0	
Spain[10]														27.2	30.4	
Sweden														65.0	69.0	
Turkey[11]														12.3		
United Kingdom[12]											26.0		33.0	39.0	46.0	
United States[13]				14.4	15.2				24.1			36.6	42.1		51.0	56.5
Percentage of individuals with a home PC																
Netherlands[14]	10.0	11.0	14.0	18.0	21.0	25.0	29.0	31.0	34.0	39.0	43.0	47.0	55.0			
Netherlands[15]												55.0	59.2	66.0	70.0	74.0
Norway									33.0	39.0	43.0	50.0	57.0	67.0	71.0	
Portugal														24.1	29.0	

1. February of each year, except for 2000, average of the year.
2. May of each year. Household Facilities and equipment Survey.
3. Survey of Household Spending.
4. June of each year.
5. For 1999, Multipurpose statistical survey on household: Everyday life aspects. For 2000, Multipurpose statistical survey on household: the citizens and their leisure – year 2000. ISTAT provisional data.
6. Fiscal year ending in March. Economic and Planning Agency.
7. Fiscal year ending in March. Ministry of Posts and Telecommunications, Communications usage trend survey.
8. Households in urban areas with more than 15 000 inhabitants only.
9. March of each year. 1999 and 2000 are projections.
10. Provisional data
11. Households in urban areas only.
12. Last quarter 2000.
13. November of each year, except August for 2000 and September 2001.
14. From CBS, Sociaal-economish panelonderzoek.
15. From CBS, POLS survey.
Source: OECD, ICCP, compiled from National Statistical Offices or national official sources.

Table 6. **Households with access to Internet[1] in selected OECD countries, 1996-2001**

	1996	1997	1998	1999	2000	2001
Percentage of households						
Australia	4.3		15.9	22.0	33.0	
Austria					19.0	
Belgium				14.0		
Canada[2]		16.0	23.0	29.0	40.0	
Denmark	5.0	10.0	22.0	33.0	46.0	
Finland				24.7	30.0	34.6
France[3]				7.0	12.0	
Germany				11.0	16.0	
Ireland					20.4	
Italy[4]				7.7	18.8	
Japan[5]		3.3	6.4	11.0	19.1	34.0
Mexico				3.0		
Norway					48.0	55.0
Sweden				42.3	48.2	65.0
Turkey[6]					7.0	
United Kingdom[7]				20.0	33.0	36.0
United States[8]			26.2		41.5	50.5
Percentage of individuals with access at home through a PC						
Netherlands[9]			16.0	26.5	45.0	57.0

1. For Denmark, Ireland, the Netherlands and the United Kingdom, access to the Internet via a home computer; for the other countries access to the Internet through any device (*e.g.* computer, phone, TV, etc.).
2. November of each year. Regular users.
3. June of each year.
4. Percentage of Households with home Internet access, not necessarily only from a PC. Provisional data for Italy.
5. Fiscal year ending in March.
6. Households in urban areas only.
7. Fourth quarter for 1999 and 2000, third quarter for 2001.
8. November 1998, August 2000, September 2001.
9. Fall of each year.
Source: OECD, compiled from National Statistical Offices or national official sources.

Table 7. **Proportion of households with Internet access by income bracket**

		1997	1998	1999	200	2001	2002
Australia	Lowest		5.0	6.0	10.0		
	Highest		44.0	52.0	69.0		
Canada	Lowest	5.5	7.1	10.9	16.5		
	Highest	32.5	44.9	53.5	65.4		
Denmark	Lowest				26.0		
	Highest				67.8		
Finland	Lowest		4.0	9.6	11.6	15.0	20.0
	Highest		36.8	50.2	64.0	69.2	69.4
France	Lowest			2.1	3.5		
	Highest			32.1	51.1		
Japan	Lowest			5.5	21.1		
	Highest			36.7	58.8		
Norway	Lowest					22.0	
	Highest					77.0	
United Kingdom	Lowest			1.0	5.0	8.0	
	Highest			32.0	62.0	78.0	
Proportion of Individuals with Internet access by income bracket							
Netherlands	Lowest		4.9	7.0			
	Highest		37.5	57.2			
United States	Lowest	9.2	13.7		18.9	25.0	
	Highest	44.5	58.9		70.1	78.9	

Note: Income brackets are defined as follows:

Australia: Lowest income bracket: less than AUD 25 000; highest income bracket: more than AUD 100 000.

Canada: Lowest income bracket: first income quartile; highest income bracket: fourth income quartile.

Denmark: Lowest income bracket: 100 000-199 999 Danish KR; highest income bracket: 400 000 Danish KR. or more.

Finland: Lowest income bracket: first income quartile; highest income bracket: fourth income quartile.

France: Lowest income bracket: less than FRF 80 000; highest income bracket: more than FRF 450 000.

Japan: Lowest income bracket: less than JPY 4 million; highest income bracket: more than JPY 20 million for 1999, more than JPY 10 million for 2000.

Norway: Lowest income bracket: less than NOK 259 000; highest income bracket: more than NOK 600 000.

United Kingdom: Lowest income bracket: second decile of income; Highest income bracket: Tenth income decile.

Netherlands: Lowest income bracket: second income decile; highest income bracket: tenth income decile.

United States: Lowest income bracket: less than USD 15 000; highest income bracket: more than USD 75 000.

Source: OECD ICT database (March 2002), and national sources.

Table 8. **Growth of household Internet access**

		1997-1998	1998-1999	1999-2000	2000-2001
Growth of Households with Internet access by income bracket					
Australia	Lowest		20%	67%	
	Highest		18%	33%	
Canada	Lowest	29%	54%	51%	
	Highest	38%	19%	22%	
Denmark	Lowest				
	Highest				
Finland	Lowest		140%	21%	29%
	Highest		36%	27%	8%
France	Lowest			67%	
	Highest			59%	
Japan	Lowest			284%	
	Highest			60%	
United Kingdom	Lowest			400%	60%
	Highest			94%	26%
Growth of Individuals with Internet access by income bracket					
Netherlands	Lowest			44%	
	Highest			53%	
United States	Lowest	49%			32%
	Highest	32%			13%

Note: Income brackets are defined as follows:

Australia: Lowest income bracket: less than AUD 25 000; highest income bracket: more than AUD 100 000.

Canada: Lowest income bracket: first income quartile; highest income bracket: fourth income quartile.

Denmark: Lowest income bracket: 100 000-199 999 Danish KR; highest income bracket: 400 000 Danish KR. or more.

Finland: Lowest income bracket: first income quartile; highest income bracket: fourth income quartile.

France: Lowest income bracket: less than FRF 80 000; highest income bracket: more than FRF 450 000.

Japan: Lowest income bracket: less than JPY 4 million; highest income bracket: more than JPY 20 million for 1999, more than JPY 10 million for 2000.

United Kingdom: Lowest income bracket: second decile of income; Highest income bracket: tenth income decile.

Netherlands: Lowest income bracket: second income decile; highest income bracket: tenth income decile.

United States: Lowest income bracket: less than USD 15 000; highest income bracket: more than USD 75 000.

Source: OECD ICT database (March 2002), and US Department of Commerce A Nation Online, 2002

Table 9. **Internet home access among households by income quartile,* 2000**

(%)

	Household Internet access	First income quartile	Fourth income quartile
Australia	33.0	9.0	58.0
Canada	40.1	16.5	65.4
Denmark[1]	52.0	37.0	53.0
Finland	30.0	11.6	64.0
Turkey[2]	6.9	0.1	21.4
United Kingdom[3]	33.0	4.0	41.0
United States	41.5	14.0	77.0

*   For Denmark, the Netherlands and the United Kingdom, access to the Internet via a home computer; for the other countries access to the Internet through any device (*e.g.* computer, phone, TV, etc.).

1. First quarter 2001.
2. Households in urban areas only.
3. Last quarter 2000.

Source: OECD, ICT database.

OECD PUBLICATIONS, 2, rue André-Pascal, 75775 PARIS CEDEX 16
PRINTED IN FRANCE
(42 2003 07 1 P) ISBN 92-64-10117-9 – No. 53033 2003